USING YOUR HEAD

USING
YOUR HEAD

The Many Ways
of Being Smart

SARA GILBERT

Macmillan Publishing Company / New York

Macmillan Publishing Company
866 Third Avenue, New York, N.Y. 10022
Collier Macmillan Canada, Inc.
Printed in the United States of America
10 9 8 7 6 5 4 3 2 1

Library of Congress Cataloging in Publication Data
Gilbert, Sara D.
Using your head.
Bibliography: p.
Includes index.
Summary: Discusses what it means to be smart, how
intelligence and talent vary from one person to another,
and how to make the best of the brain you have.
1. Intellect—Juvenile literature. 2. Left and
right (Psychology)—Juvenile literature. 3. Cerebral
dominance—Juvenile literature. [1. Intellect.
2. Ability. 3. Thought and thinking. 4. Brain]
I. Title.
BF431.G533 1984   153   84–9736
ISBN 0–02–736720–7

For S.D.G. from S.D.G.,
with pride and love

Contents

USING YOUR HEAD

(1)

How Smart Are You?

"Jennifer is the smartest kid in the class." What do her classmates mean when they say that? Probably that she gets the best grades on all the tests. That indeed may be one sign of being "smart," and you very likely have a good idea of who among your classmates, friends, and relatives is the smartest.

By about the fifth grade, most people have become aware that they are better at some skills than their friends are, or that some of their classmates are smarter than they are. The question: "How smart am I?" takes on more meaning as you grow through the years of junior high or intermediate school and on toward high school and beyond. That is not only because grades, which many people view as a sign of intelligence, take on added meaning with each school year. It is also because "How smart am I?" is part of the bigger question young people find themselves asking: "Who am I?"

How smart you feel you are can play a big role in how you feel about your*self*—and your ideas about yourself guide how and what you do in all areas of your life. So, in order to become all that you can be in the future, it is especially important that you know as much as you can now about what being smart means.

It used to be that only people who did well on tests of various kinds were called "smart." Many who still think that way, though, make a mistake. They forget about the talents of people who don't get such good grades. They also show that they don't understand all the ways of "using your head."

For instance, is Steve, who has memorized the records of every major league baseball player since 1950, smart?

What about Sally, who gets pretty good grades without much work because she knows just how to smile at the teacher: Is she smart?

Or Jason, who's already earned enough money to buy his own stereo and video game: Is he smart?

Is Phyllis, who tries to squeeze schoolwork in while training six hours a day toward becoming an Olympic swimmer, smart?

Alex is an artist who sometimes gets so wrapped up in his own projects that he forgets to do his homework. Is he smart?

How about Kim, who came to this country only last year and gets rotten grades, but already speaks English with ease: Is he smart?

Or Andrea, who hates school but organized an

entire musical show, from tickets and posters to scenery and dance steps: Is she smart?

All of those people are using their heads—and using what is inside of the head: the brain.

A Look Inside

Human beings are probably the only creatures who use their minds to try to understand their minds: People throughout history, and perhaps before, have been fascinated by how we think, know, do, and remember what we do. By about 2,500 years ago, at least some people had realized that the brain was the organ that performed those functions, but until modern times, they were able only to imagine, theorize, and philosophize about what goes on inside our heads.

Even relatively modern scientists, though, could examine the insides of heads only from the outside or by taking apart the brains removed from dead bodies —*after* they had ceased to function. By several centuries ago, doctors had made a good start on determining what role the brain plays in the regulation of the body's physical activities—sensing, respiration, circulation, and so forth—but without being able to examine working brains, they could only guess at the connections between the brain and such activities of "the mind" as thought, feeling, and intelligence. In the late 1700s, for instance, some scientists had decided that certain mental skills were concentrated in certain specific parts of the brain, so during the 1800s, people were convinced that bumps in different parts of the skull indicated different levels of intelligence and talent. Using the techniques of "phrenology," as this pseudoscience was known, they would literally "have their heads examined" for the bumps that supposedly indicated strengths in such areas as memory, ambition, or will power. Though this theory was rather quickly shown to be false, a related (and also false) idea—that the weight and size of the brain and its various parts were signs of intelligence—continued well into the twentieth century.

More productive research during the 1700s and 1800s began to detail the system of electrical connections that operate the brain and the nervous system and to pinpoint the centers of activity in the brain. These findings, based upon studies of animals, corpses, and, occasionally, brain-damaged individuals, led to the development of the concept that "madness," or insanity, was a "disorder of the nerves." From that point, near the opening of the twentieth century, psychology, which had previously been more philosophy than science, began to focus on the relationship between the brain's activities and human behavior. Some early psychologists, beginning with the most famous, Sigmund Freud, concentrated on ways to cure diseases of the mind. Others, starting with Alfred Binet, worked on scientific ways of measuring intelligence.

Still, the brain and its functions could not be studied directly when in action. By early in this century, surgeons had found ways to stimulate electrically various parts of a person's brain and observe the resulting response, but it was only with the refinement of X rays, delicate but powerful electron microscopes, and precise chemical techniques in the middle of this century that it has been possible to get a firsthand look at how a living human brain works. Chapter 2 will summarize some of the latest information scientists have found.

Paralleling the increasing knowledge of the brain as a physical object has been a growing understanding of the brain activity we know as the mind: Chapter 3 will detail some of the most recent ideas on how we think and learn. One result of the new knowledge about the brain is the understanding that being smart means many different things. This book will tell you what science knows (and what it does not know) about overall intelligence, which is the ability to use one's head to learn, to understand, or to deal with new and unfamiliar situations.

Once, it was thought that intelligence could be measured as accurately as height or weight and rated with a precise number (called an "intelligence quotient" or "IQ"). Now, it is known that intelligence is much trickier to analyze than the height, weight, or other physical characteristics of a person.

That is because although the brain is part of the physical body, and intelligence is in some ways physically generated, many other factors go into the procedures by which we acquire and use our intelligence. Also, our brains are responsible for many skills and attributes that are hard to measure, since our creativity, our feelings, and our abilities to deal with people, to organize ourselves, and to overcome obstacles all also involve using our heads.

Identity and IQ

Brain researchers now believe that what goes on among the billions of tiny cells inside our heads produces not simply ideas and actions, but the broadest of our thoughts and the deepest of our feelings. Those thoughts and feelings lead to behaviors that in turn create for others and for ourselves an *identity*—a picture of who each of us is.

Andrea, for instance, might gain an identity as a competent, well-organized person. She might use those ideas about herself to achieve other goals, such as getting better grades, or she might downplay her own skills while envying the school success of someone like Jennifer.

Or Kim might look to all he has *not* achieved,

rather than use pride in his quick language success as the spur to other achievements.

. . . And so forth: Intelligence and talent—and especially the ways in which we use them—probably have as much to do with personal background and attitudes as they do with brain power.

How smart are *you?* How are you *smart?* And, how can you make best use of your kind of smarts?

In this book, you will be able to explore the answers to those important questions.

Answers and Questions

We will begin with some of the latest available information about how the human brain works, because to use your head, you need to know what goes on inside it and why.

We will also look into why and how intelligence is different for different people. You can find out here about the many talents and abilities, besides IQ, that a person needs or can use, so that you can gain an understanding of your particular brand of intelligence.

Then, you can work some tests and riddles to help you discover and develop the best ways for you to use *your* head, and read some suggestions for doing just that.

Finally, you'll find a reminder of why it's both

possible and important to exercise all the many parts of your brain and your intelligence, along with a list of books in the back that will help you to keep stretching your mind. (Also in the back, beginning on page 117, are definitions of some of the less familiar words you may bump into as you read.)

This book won't give you all the answers about who you are or what it means to be smart: Science is coming up with new information every day about being smart; besides, it is only *your* brain that can pinpoint exactly who you are. But it will give as many answers as possible and, perhaps more importantly, will start you asking questions—which, after all, is the only way to find answers to anything!

We will, however, start off with a few answers to the questions about Jennifer, Steve, Sally, Jason, Phyllis, Alex, Kim, and Andrea on pages 1 to 3. Are they smart?

Of course they are—each in his or her own way. So are most people, in some style or another, and in this book we are going to call those styles "book smarts," "art smarts," "street smarts," "body smarts," and "people smarts."

Keep those names and identities from pages 1 to 3 in mind, because you'll be meeting them throughout the book, as we explore the meaning to you of the different forms and sources of intelligence.

And now for some more questions.

This is a big one: What *is* intelligence?

Is it the sum of an almost countless number of buzzing connections taking place within a small organ inside the skull?

Is it a mysterious quality, like "mind" or "soul," that appears from an unknown source?

Is it a definite object, born into us and derived from our ancestors?

Does it grow with us, starting as nothing and developing within our environment as our bodies do?

Is it:

All of the above?
Some of the above?
None of the above?

The answer to the big one, if a single answer exists, lies within the brain—so let's take a look inside your head.

(2)

What's Inside Your Head?

"She sure is brainy," you might say about the smartest kid in your class. Or, "He's got brains," or, "What a brain!"

The truth is, of course, that it's not just successful students who "have brains." Alex the artist and Phyllis the athlete have brains, just as Jennifer "the brain" does—we all do, and the function of that small organ inside each skull determines what we do, how we feel, and what we are good at, so it's important to know what the brain does and how.

Your brain started functioning before you were born, but only in a very minimal fashion, and it's taken quite a while for it to develop to the point where it is capable of understanding abstract concepts. One such concept is the idea that a physical mass like the brain can create abstractions like thoughts, dreams, and fantasies.

By receiving and sending signals from and to all parts of the nervous system, some areas of the brain control such all-important bodily activities as breathing, heartbeat, digestion, and other "involuntary" life-support functions that go on even when you are asleep or unconscious. Other areas allow you to make such "voluntary" movements as walking or grasping. Still others keep you, through your senses, in touch with the world.

Scientists have long been able to pinpoint the brain's role in these basics, but only fairly recently have their complex, computerized techniques and equipment been able to explore the ways in which brain cells control and create thoughts, feelings, drives, moods, behaviors—all of those characteristics that give humans a special quality and make individual humans unique.

Building a Brain

Your brain probably looks much like those your friends are carrying around inside their skulls, and much like those of adults: By the age of seven, most brains have grown to their full size and weight.

But the brain doesn't look like much: Its appearance has been described as like that of porridge or dirty gelatin. If you mixed some cold cooked oatmeal with plain gelatin and poured it into a bowl about the size of your skull, when you unmolded it, you'd have a pretty good idea of what your brain looks (and feels) like. To get an idea of its weight, keep your imagination in the kitchen: At about three pounds, the brain weighs about as much as a family pack of ground beef.

To achieve an even more realistic-looking brain model, we would line the mold with creased aluminum foil, with one large, straight ridge down the middle. We'd add some extra oatmeal to part of the gelatin, line the mold with about one-quarter inch of that, and let it set before we poured in the rest. When firm and unmolded, this goop would appear to have the crevices and fissures and the two "halves" of the real thing. Slice a cross section, and you would see an outer layer much denser than the inner core. In an actual brain, there are reasons for these different shapes and densities.

The crevices are created when the brain folds over on itself. A human brain must grow to maximum size within the limited space allowed by the solid, bony structure of its protective covering, the skull. Humans, over the eons, have packed more information systems into their brains than other animals, and since the organ can't expand the skull, it must grow by doubling back on itself. The size and weight of anyone's brain depends largely on the size of his or her body, and the relatively small variations in that size have little or nothing to do with differences in intelligence.

When compared with other animals, though, humans have large brains in relation to their body size, and that is one sign of their superior intelligence.

Whales and elephants, for instance, have larger brains, but *much* larger bodies. Birds' and small monkeys' brains make up a larger percentage of their body weight than humans', but those animals' bodies are much smaller than humans'. The brain-to-body ratio of dolphins and apes is closest to that of humans —an indication of their intelligence possibilities, since millions of years of human evolution have produced a brain that has packed the greatest possible capability into the smallest possible space.

If the human skull were large enough to contain an "unfolded" brain, people would be overly top-heavy creatures, and birth would be very difficult and complicated. As it is, babies, whose bodies are only one-twentieth of adult size at birth, are born with brains one-fourth their full size. Infant brains are housed in skulls that are almost half the size of their bodies and whose bones are still soft enough to squeeze through the birth canal.

As much as possible of the brain's development goes on before birth, but a human baby has to wait until it is out of the confining space of the womb before full growth can occur. The development process inside the womb has a lot to do with the different layers inside our heads, and it also reflects the entire human evolutionary process.

After only three weeks, the nerve cells in the embryo have started to differentiate into three sections along a curved tube. At the bottom is what will become the brain stem, or hindbrain, the most basic part of the brain, which we share with all living creatures. In the middle are the cells forming the beginnings of the midbrain, the center generally for our emotions and "instincts," a portion we have in common with animals who have climbed partway up the evolutionary ladder. Around the curve at the top of the tube are specialized cells that multiply rapidly into ever-larger double loops as they form the forebrain, which is well developed only in the higher orders of animals.

By about four months after conception, development is in progress on the brain's outer section, the neocortex, or "new layer," which becomes the most complex part of the brain and which is better developed in humans than in any other creatures. (It is this layer that appears in our jellied model as the outer shell more densely filled with oatmeal.) At about the same point in development, a groove between the two portions of the forebrain becomes apparent (aluminum foil made it in the jellied mold), dividing the two highly specialized sections called hemispheres that characterize the human brain and provide us with mental skills unmatched by any other animals.

When human babies are born, their brains contain almost as many cells as they ever will—yet, especially when compared with the young of other species, they are helpless to care for themselves for a long time after birth.

Those two facts indicate that what you *see* when you look at that wrinkly mold of "jellied oatmeal" is a lot less than what you've got inside your head.

Making Connections

What you've *got* is the possibility for an almost infinite number of connections between and among the 10 to 100 *billion* cells that make up the organ called the brain. A newborn baby has only just begun to make those connections. With everything you do, learn, remember, sense, or feel, you connect more cells, so that even when the physical growth of your brain stops, its development continues, creating networks of neurons when you use your head.

Neurons are nerve cells. You have as many as 8 billion of them in the thin neocortex layer alone, and outside the brain billions more form "wires" that carry messages back and forth between the brain and every part of the body, triggering actions and reactions within the messy mass inside your skull. Just as the plain outside of a computer gives no clue to the microelectronic maze inside, so the uninspiring gray look of the brain disguises intricate circuits that science has only recently begun to trace.

Scientists have long known that nerve cells are different from other cells in the body, and that brain cells are a specialized form of nerve cells: That is easy enough to determine by examination with a simple microscope. Today, through the use of much more sensitive microscopes attached to camera lenses, of computer-controlled measuring devices, of radioactive blood tracings and other marvels created by the human brain they study, scientists are discovering even more delicate specializations among nerve cells. This specialization allows for almost incredibly precise interactions among the cells in the brain.

In this book, we can only begin to explore some of those interactions, but we have to make at least that beginning, because within those billions of neurons and their connections are the keys to your many ways of being smart.

Anything you do that requires brain activity—and that is *everything* you do—requires a series of electro-

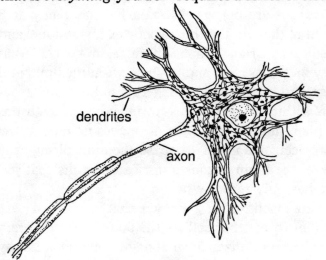

dendrites

axon

chemical chain reactions. That long word simply means that electrical signals are sent between nerve cells by passing through one of the various chemicals that exist naturally in the brain. Here's how the process works.

Neurons are unusual cells. The body of each one branches out into fibers called axons and dendrites. The dendrites are covered by hairlike spines, which receive signals from neighboring neurons and then pass them to the cell body, where they are then transmitted along the axons to other surrounding cells. The signals take the form of electrical impulses created by the chemical properties of the different fluids filling and surrounding each cell. (The batteries that operate your portable radio or cassette player create electricity in exactly the same way.)

The point at which each axon relays its message to each spine on a neighboring dendrite is called a "synapse," which is a tiny gap between the two cells that contains chemicals that transmit the signal. The type of chemical that fills any given synapse determines the nature of the signal being sent, and different portions of the brain, it now appears, have developed different sorts of neurons and chemicals.

Which Department?

Throughout most of the several thousand years that humans have been studying the human brain, they have assumed that the different sections controlled different activities. Though some of the early ideas—that "common sense" was located in a particular cortex, for instance—seem foolish today, scientific research has shown that those original assumptions were correct: The brain does divide its labor among its various segments.

For instance, when you breathe or digest your lunch, or every time your heart pumps out a fresh pulse of blood to nourish all your body's cells, you call unconsciously on the control centers located in the brain stem or hindbrain (see the drawing below).

On a hot day you sweat, and on a cold day the

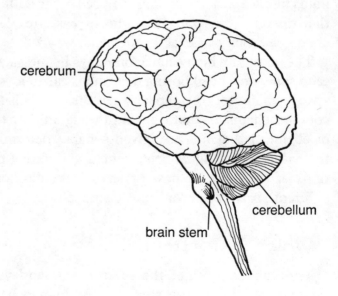

body's "thermostat" in the thyroid gland raises your internal temperature, thanks to the hypothalamus, a large cluster of cells in the midbrain that also lets you know, without your realizing it, when you are thirsty or hungry, happy or depressed. The thalamus, near-by, allows your muscles to move in response to the messages from your senses. The pituitary gland controls, among other things, the release of hormones that allow your body to produce energy from the food you eat, and the tiny pineal gland, right smack in the middle of the brain mass, is responsible for the rate at which your body grows and matures.

While basic functions like these are obviously important, it is in the forebrain that the activities we most commonly associate with the brain take place. Occupying the largest portion of the forebrain is the *cerebrum,* which is a Latin word meaning simply "brain." Its sections—lobes, cortices, and other units —contain different networks of cells that control our most important conscious activities.

For some examples of how those controls work, let's think again of the "smart kids" introduced in Chapter 1.

When Alex the artist sees a scene that he would like to paint, for instance, an electrochemical signal shoots along the optic nerve from his eye into the visual cortex near the back of his head.

To learn his new language, Kim used cells in the

frontal, temporal, and parietal lobes on the left side of the cerebrum.

Steve calls on cells within his temporal and frontal lobes to trigger the facts he's memorized about all those baseball players.

Phyllis's athletic training has developed a strong network of cells in the motor cortex, near the top of the head, that controls her swimming strokes.

When Andrea begins to organize a show, she triggers a chain reaction in the "planning centers" of the frontal lobes.

And when Jennifer, Jason, or Sally—or anyone— thinks, they set buzzing the dense networks of cells in the cerebral cortex, which coordinate electrochemical signals sent to them from all parts of the brain at once.

Another important coordinating center lies in the *corpus callosum* ("hard body"), which connects the two hemispheres ("half globes") of the forebrain. This central section is a dense network of nerves— communication cables that pass information between the two sides. Why two sides? The answer to that is not certain, except that humans are by nature "bilateral" creatures: We are among those species that tend to be balanced on both sides of the body, with right limbs that match left limbs, an eye on each side of the face, and so forth. It may be that the brain simply follows that pattern.

Early brain research showed that each hemisphere

in general controlled the opposite side of the body. The actions of your right hand, for example, are guided by neurons in the left side of your brain; visual images received through your left eye are decoded by activity in the right hemisphere, and the connecting nerves coordinate the operations.

In most people, even the left-handed, the left cerebral hemisphere is dominant: Our right eyes are more acute than our left, for instance, and left-handed people tend to be adept in some skills with their right hands. Why this should be true is not known, but when neuroscientists began to be able to probe deeply into living brains, they discovered some other right-side/left-side dominances. The left side seemed to be completely in charge of such complex abilities as speech, reading, writing, and mathematics, while the right side handled spatial relationships, abstractions, and tactile perceptions. From those discoveries came the concept that the left side of the forebrain represented a person's analytical, rational, and controlled aspects, while the right side controlled the artistic, emotional, or spiritual qualities. Therefore, went the thinking, individual personality characteristics might depend on the dominance of one side of the brain or the other. An artist like Alex would be "right brained" and a methodical, studious person like Jennifer would be "left brained."

But it seems that the brain is more complicated than that. Research in the early 1980s indicated that,

although the cells managing those different intellectual activities are concentrated in different hemispheres of the brain, they are also scattered throughout other portions of it. The brain may compute
different forms of mathematics, for instance, in various sections: multiplication in one area and division
in another. Reading requires a variety of mental activities, each of which takes place in different areas of
the forebrain.

Wherever it is that the specific activities of the
brain take place, it seems that the type of response
depends in part on the delicate variations in the types
of nerve cells involved, and in part on the nature of
the chemical that fills a given synapse. The brain is
able to keep track of the multiple reactions that even
the simplest action requires. A signal picked up by
the nerves leading from the eye, for instance, will go,
at the very least, to the visual centers for decoding,
to a memory center for interpretation, and to a mo-
tor-control center to trigger more signals to stimulate
action.

Running a Program

To get an idea of how all these electrochemical
processes work, imagine that a piece of your favorite
cake is placed before your eyes. Billions of cells go
into action: seeing it, interpreting it ("cake, good"),

causing your mouth to water or your stomach to feel hungry, making you feel happiness, and extending your hand and arm to take the cake. Or, if an armed robber leaps before your eyes in a dark alley, the chain reaction would go from sight to "danger, bad," to a feeling of fear, and the rapid movement of your legs in a direction away from the robber.

Seems simple enough, doesn't it? But remember, a lot of different activities are going on inside your head at once. Think for a moment about all that you are doing right now:

Reading, which involves vision, recognition, decoding, language, memory, and imaginative visualizing;

Sitting or lying down, and probably jiggling some part of your body, which require muscular control;

Listening to music or to the other sounds around you, which involves its own set of nerves and control centers;

Feeling some emotion, which arises from your midbrain;

Being conscious of your environment and your physical state, whether there's enough light, or you're hungry, or your head aches;

Thinking, not only about the book, but probably about several other things as well;

and . . . breathing, digesting, circulating blood, regulating body temperature—all of which involve brain-cell business you're not even aware of.

And that's not *all* of the things your brain is doing for you right now.

Billions and billions of cells in your brain are sending infinitesimal signals through your head at a rate of speed impossible to imagine. Each of the billions of cells in your brain has thousands of possible connector points, and most of them are in action every instant. Doesn't that make your scalp tingle or your head buzz just a bit? Especially when you realize that every action and reaction, even the tiniest and the most unconscious, has to be broken down into its smallest bits, and then those bits have to be put back together to form a whole, all in a flash. No wonder it is said that even the most sophisticated computer is no match for the human brain! And the computer in your skull has no "down time": It's plugged in even when you are asleep.

You Are Brainy

Your brain has been running nonstop for a long time, too. When you were born, most of those neurons and synapses were already in place. Before you were born, the neurons that managed your basic life functions were in action, as were some of those that moved your muscles and limbs. But there was little else going on.

Although we all may have memories and perceptions from before birth stored away somewhere in our brains, as soon as you hit the world, you really began to learn. Perceptions that your senses picked up from the world around you and feelings, both physical and emotional, that you experienced within your small body all triggered signals within your brain, some to be stored in memory cells, others to create actions that got responses, which, in turn, caused more learning.

But if your brain is so smart, how come you don't remember all those early experiences? There are probably several answers to that one, among them:

An important part of memory is forgetting; if we remembered everything that ever happened, our memory cells would be too cluttered to retain newer information.

The *corpus callosum* is one of the last parts of the brain to become fully developed, so it may not have been on tap to convey experiences from one part of the brain to another.

An important part of interpreting the world and storing information about it is the use of language, so until you had developed skills with the verbal code, you may not have been able to hold on to many of your experiences.

Or the record of your earliest days and months may be tucked away in some cluster of the brain cells that you've grown up with, but is so deeply buried that digging it up is too difficult a process.

It's likely that most or all of your experiences are locked somewhere within your brain cells, because neuroscientists believe that each time we learn something new, even the tiniest bit, or byte, of information, a new connection is made and the brain is *changed* as one more axon locks on to one more dendrite across a chemical-filled synapse. Any time you're not feeling too "brainy," try to imagine how much you have learned in your lifetime—not simply the knowledge that you have put there on purpose, but every piece of sensory perception, every memory or emotional response, everything. Staggering, isn't it? And someone your age has only just begun: You have many more years—and countless more synapses —to build up networks in your brain.

In fact, you may well be at the *best* time in your life for learning. By the time most people have gotten a little way into adolescence, their brains have long since reached their full cellular growth, are being washed with chemicals similar to those of an adult, and have a lot of unconnected nerve cells just waiting to lock in new skills and information. Now is the best time to do it!

Research shows that in different people, different areas of the brain are better connected than in others. Because you are unique and have been around for a while, your brain already has its own special strengths, so now is also the best time to work toward your own special way of being smart.

(3)

What Do You Know?

You've already learned a lot more than you realize, because brains are always busy.

When street-smart Jason calculates the ideal way to mow a neighbor's lawn so that it takes the least possible effort to earn his pay . . . When Andrea convinces the principal to let her club use the gym for a party . . . When Phyllis figures out how to combine her science project with her swimming practice . . . they are all using their heads to do what the human brain does better than any other creature's: thinking and learning.

No matter what it is that you do well—or wish you could do better—you need to put your brain into action to think and learn. Both of these processes are so complex—involving the "higher-level" activities of the cells in the cerebral cortex as well as the buzzing background in the brain's other centers—that they can't yet be pinpointed as precisely as simpler functions. But it is possible to break them down into their steps, so that you can see what it takes to use your head for anything.

I Think ...

One way to look at the process we call thought is that it takes:

planning, perceiving, remembering, imaging, feeling, and acting.

To understand thinking in this way, pretend that you need to catch a bus. Believe it or not, that's a behavior that takes "intelligence," a high order of brain function, and here's some of what goes into it.

Planning: You need to think ahead—about bus schedules and the time it takes to reach the stop, about the money you'll need, and about clothing to suit the weather, among other things. The ability to think ahead and plan is centered in the cells of the frontal lobes of your brain.

Remembering: If you couldn't remember where the bus stop was, you'd have to find it anew each time you wanted to go there. Without memory, you'd have to learn about dressing, money, words—everything —every day. Memory is a vital part of thought, and we seem to have three types. One is *temporary*, holding perceptions only long enough for the brain to make sense of them. Without this, we couldn't focus on the letters in a word long enough to read it or keep track of what we saw before and after we blinked our eyes. Then there's *short-term* memory, probably located at the back, sides, and top of the cerebrum, where we keep track of such things as telephone numbers or words in a sentence for only as long as we need them. When we "rehearse" short-term memories, by repeating them either mentally or actually, we force them into our *long-term* memory cells in various parts of the cortex and in the midbrain. A censoring system sorts out what is important to store and what can be discarded, so that our memories don't get overcrowded; recall processes allow us to bring necessary memories into consciousness. In these ways, you can remember how to find the bus stop without having to think about it all the time.

Perceiving: Your senses feed your brain the raw material for your thoughts. If you couldn't see where you were going, you wouldn't know where to turn for the bus stop; if you couldn't feel the change in your pocket, you'd have trouble deciding how much to take out; if you couldn't sense depth or judge speed, you wouldn't know whether you'd have to run or walk to the bus stop. Information from your eyes goes to cells in the visual cortex at the top of the head; cells that sense touch are in the parietal lobe nearby; and the ears send nerve signals to the temporal lobe on the side of the cerebrum. People whose sensory systems have been damaged develop ways to compensate.

Their brains develop new pathways for the signals. If no signals can be sent, as in the case of total deafness or blindness, the cells that interpret impressions from healthy senses make new, stronger connections, sharpening other senses.

Imaging: If you were to describe the way you think, you would probably mention "seeing pictures" or "hearing words," or both, inside your head. This kind of imaging, as that process is called, flashes across so many billions of cells in your brain so fast that if you were to try to report every word or scene that you are mentally hearing or seeing at this very instant, it would probably take an hour.

As you walk to the bus stop, the images flashing through your head might include: the scene of the bus stop you're headed for, a memory of the times you've had to wait forever for the bus or one when you've had to run to catch it, an image of the bus approaching the stop, and what number it displays on the front.

Language is an important shorthand for communicating experiences, and mental "language" is a vital shortcut for thought. By condensing all of our experiences, perceptions, memories, plans, and actions into a fast code, internal language increases the speed of our thoughts and behavior. By plugging the brain's language centers (mostly in the left hemisphere) into your bus-catching project, you can use unspoken words to turn your image of the bus approaching the stop and your memory of running for it into quick action.

Feeling: Our emotions arise from our brains as well. From cells clustered in the brain stem and in the hypothalamus, which is buried deep inside the forebrain, come signals that trigger the body chemicals that in turn produce the whole range of human feelings. Those feelings, of course, influence the way we think and act: If your images of the bus ride or of the school day that follows it make you unhappy, you are likely to go more slowly to the bus stop than if you were happily looking forward to a party with friends. Feelings motivated—got you started on—your trip to the bus stop in the first place. Perhaps it was a feeling of fear about getting into trouble if you were late once more, or a feeling of pride because you were going to turn in a project that you had worked hard on.

Action: Most thought leads to action of some kind. (*I see a car coming fast; I know that if it hit me it could hurt me; I will step back onto the curb.*) Of course, the brain controls those actions. Thinking leads at least to another thought: How many thoughts are you having right now? What word in the last sentence triggered a memory that made you think of something else that has nothing to do with either this book or with walking to a bus stop?

For while you are going to catch a real bus, with your brain automatically piecing together all of the elements of the thought processes that will get you to your goal, you are also thinking and feeling about a variety of other topics. And it's all going on at the same time, in one instant after another. How well all those elements of thinking function together determines, in part, how smart or intelligent a person is.

Jason's money-making ability, Andrea's people sense, and Phyllis's swimming skill all depend on the same step-by-step processes that combine to create thought.

What is something that you are very good at doing? Stop for a moment and think about the planning, perceiving, remembering, imaging, feeling, and acting that combine to allow you to do it.

...Therefore, I Learn

And how did you get to be good at your specialty? You learned—perhaps by making a conscious effort to learn, or perhaps without realizing that you were learning at all. But everything we do or know, we have learned. When we think, we make use of brain-cell connections that already exist. When we learn, we are linking up new connections.

At the very simplest level, connections are linked —learning takes place—through a process of *stimulus, response,* and *reward.* A hungry rat accidentally presses a lever in its cage, and a pellet of food is released. Soon the rat has *learned* to press the lever in order to get food: The sight, or perception, of the lever *stimulates* the rat to *respond* to receive the *reward* of food. In humans, too, learning follows that process, but it becomes almost infinitely complex because the possible stimuli, responses, and rewards are so varied and complex. In fact, in humans, the ability to learn is a big part of what we call intelligence, and in general, except for those forms of basic, perception-response learning that we share with other animals, we learn by problem solving of some sort or another.

To solve a problem, whether in math class or on an unfamiliar street, you go through these steps:

Seeing the problem
Comparing it with similar ones you've encountered and noting the differences
Deciding what information you need to solve it
Calling on your memory and inventive powers to come up with what you need
Planning your steps
Taking the action you've decided on
Judging whether your system worked or not
Storing the experience in your memory

Let's solve the imaginary problem of finding a bus you need in a town with which you are unfamiliar. That might not seem too tough, but in solving it, you'll combine the basic ingredients of the thought process into a special blend that produces a problem-solving system.

You recognize that you may have difficulty in finding an unfamiliar bus stop, and you realize that, although you know the basic steps, this particular task will take some extra time and effort, so you plan your action further in advance than you would in your regular routine.

Deciding that you will need directions to the bus stop as well as information about fares and route numbers (since you remember that these are important ingredients), you call on your skill with language and your knowledge of information sources to find what you need from an expert or a map.

With those directions in your mind, you visualize or imagine the actual directions and techniques you'll need to get where you're going. On your way there, your perceptions will help guide you, and mental images summoned from both long- and short-term memory will help you locate the right spot.

You'll know you've solved the problem when the bus you want stops at the place where you're waiting. And, probably without thinking about it, you'll store away the successful techniques (and the mistakes), making new connections or strengthening old ones in your brain, so that the next time you go to a strange bus stop, or any other new place, you will have the pattern readily available.

By using your head to solve the problem, you have

learned something new—not just about finding your way, but about problem solving itself—and that learning makes other learning simpler. Different people might take different approaches to solving the problem of how to get from here to there in a strange place. A book-oriented person like Jennifer would be likely to use a map and a bus schedule, while people-centered Andrea would find the best person to ask. Artistic Alex might follow his creative nose to the place that seems most likely, based on his observations, while Jason the hustler could easily give up on finding the stop and hitchhike, instead. Each of us has our own *style* of learning, but in general, the process follows the same steps.

Do you have to be smart to find a bus stop? You might not think so, but it's the sort of task that very young children, whose brain cells are not well connected, or people whose brains are damaged or insufficiently developed, need special training to accomplish. And imagine how pleased you would be with yourself if you got onto the right bus in a foreign city where you didn't speak the language!

You don't think of tying your shoes, making change, or even reading as signs of being smart, either, and yet they all had to be learned, and they are all acts guided by intelligence. Like anything else that requires thought, they all involve planning, perceiving, remembering, imaging, feeling, and acting.

Measuring Brain Power

Of course, simply being able to think, or to perform acts slightly more complicated than those a monkey could do, does not make a person intelligent. How well we put together all the pieces of the thought or learning process equals how smart we are. But, as we've seen, those processes are complicated even in their simplest forms, and a lot of smart people have struggled for a long time to achieve a good definition of "intelligence." In fact, they're still struggling.

What do *you* mean when you say someone is smart?

Let's work our way to an answer by looking again at our examples from the first chapter, to find some of their key qualities.

Jennifer shows that she is smart by learning school-work quickly and thoroughly.

Steve is highly motivated and uses his memory well when dealing with his baseball hobby.

Sally makes good use of judgment in her management of people.

Jason displays special problem-solving ability in his business ventures.

Kim has shown great language skill in learning English so quickly.

Phyllis is a good planner and is using her mind to attain her athletic goal.

Alex is capable of raising imaging to the level of great creativity in his artwork.

When you think of your own friends and classmates, you can probably think of a few with some or all of these qualities: learning ability, motivation, memory, speed, judgment, problem-solving skill, good use of language and other symbols, and creativity.

Those ingredients combine to produce smarts in any area of life. An athlete—or an artist, a scholar, or a business whiz—needs to develop those mental abilities in order to achieve a goal.

"Goal-directed, adaptive behavior" is one of the better definitions of intelligence that researchers have come up with, especially since it applies to the ability to use one's head in almost any activity.

Being smart, then, means exercising the billions of cells in our brains to make best use of learning ability, memory, speed, judgment, problem solving, good use of symbols, and creativity toward achieving goals that we have chosen to strive for.

And how do we know how smart a person is? One way to judge is to use intelligence or "IQ" tests.

As we've said, IQ stands for "intelligence quotient." A quotient is the number resulting from the division of two other numbers. (In: "What is 4 divided by 2?" the answer, "2," is the quotient.) Once, intelligence tests were designed to measure a person's "mental age" by rating the problem-solving tasks the person was able to do against his or her actual age and dividing the two to come up with the intelligence quotient. Later, different rating scales were devised, but the term "IQ" stuck.

Intelligence testing began during the early part of this century, when the then-new knowledge about the brain and the mind seemed to indicate that intelligence might be an absolute quantity that could be measured as a thermometer measures temperature. The first tests, developed in France, were intended to identify retarded students among the country's schoolchildren. Soon afterward, during World War I, IQ tests were used to classify vast numbers of soldiers into broad categories of ability. Once these efforts seemed successful, people came to believe that tests could rate much narrower differences in mental skills. Since that time, psychologists and other researchers have worked to develop tests that are involved and accurate enough to measure that very complex and, as they have come to realize, rather fuzzy thing called intelligence.

You may have taken intelligence tests, either as part of a group in school or individually with a special tester. They are slightly different from the other kinds of tests you take in that they ask you to work as much with designs and pictures as with words and numbers. That is partly because the mental manipulation of symbols is considered an important clue to intelligence levels, and partly because the tests attempt to avoid measuring what you have already learned. In theory, a person who can't read or solve math problems should be able to come up with a score equal to that of someone with the same intelligence level who has already learned those skills.

Unfortunately, so far no one has invented an IQ test that is, in fact, fair to test-takers of all backgrounds. Though the tests aren't supposed to require learned knowledge, they actually do: Even pictures and symbols have different meanings to different people, depending on what they have learned. Also, approaches to learning and problem solving vary greatly, and it is difficult to take these differences into account when designing a single test.

As people have come to realize that these tests are not absolute measures of intelligence, they have given less weight to the importance of an IQ score. Some of the newer intelligence tests approach the problem from different directions and may produce a clearer picture of individual styles of intelligence, especially when given in combination with creativity tests and personality profiles. As modern research reveals more about the delicate rainbow of qualities that go into intelligence, more questions are raised about whether it is possible for any single test to measure it. And, although today brain scanners can reveal what our brains are doing or thinking about, as yet they cannot judge how *well* we are using our heads.

When we return to the definition of intelligence as

"goal-directed, adaptive behavior," we realize how varied intelligence can be. In other words, different people are smart in different ways, and in many ways that are difficult to measure. Even though the ingredients of intelligence are the same, the forms and combinations of those ingredients vary widely.

What accounts for the variations? Why are some people smart in one way and others in another?

We've seen that different parts of the brain control different behaviors, feelings, and interests. Brain researchers have found that the best-used parts of the brain are the most densely developed. So, some people make more use of some centers of their brains than others. We'll explore the reasons for that in the next chapter.

But first, think about your own brain: What parts would you say have the strongest linkages, and why do you think that might be?

(4)

Why Do You Know It?

If you are good at sports, you might explain that your mother or father is also good at sports. Or if you get good grades, you might say, "It's because my brothers and sisters get good grades, too."

Those explanations may well be accurate, for several reasons.

Before You Were Born...

To at least some extent, we inherit our particular ways of being smart from our parents. The two reproductive cells that unite to start the development of a baby's body within the mother's womb contain an almost incredible quantity of detailed information about the bodies of the man and the woman who parented the child. When the cells join, the chromosomes containing the genes that carry this information combine and then divide, as the two cells multiply to create a unique individual. The chromosomes and genes provide chemical "instructions" for the structure and organization of the new body, including, of course, the brain.

Both of the people who gave you life inherited their set of genes from their parents, who got them from theirs, and so forth, so that each new individual grows with a unique combination of markers to guide the development of every major and minor portion of the body. Every human being is basically similar to every other one, as you can see by looking around you, but every human being is also different from every other one in details—as you see from thinking about the people you know.

The same goes for your brain, too. Science does not yet know how specific is the "map" for the brain contained in the chromosomes, but your precise number of brain cells and the chemical fine-tuning of their organization are probably due to your inheritance, passed along not only from your parents, but from their parents and grandparents as well.

Parents can't pass along to children information or skills that they have *learned* with their brains since their own births: If they could, almost every child would know how to read, drive a car, or find a bus stop without ever having to be taught. But your brain is likely to have areas of special sensitivity similar to those of your parents. If your mother's visual cortex and creative centers are especially densely packed with cells and sensitive chemicals, for instance, yours may be, too. She may have used those physical qualities to become an artist, and you may or may not do the same. Remember that your brain also controls your emotional makeup, which will determine in large part how you make use of the programs in your brain cells. If your father's nerve patterns make for superior eye-hand coordination that allows him to be an excellent carpenter or ball player, your eye-hand skills may also be exceptional, ready to use for your own purposes.

There have long been arguments, which still continue, about how much influence this kind of heredity has on intelligence. At one extreme, some scientists maintained that genes absolutely determined intelligence. Early researchers pointed to the fact that some brains were bigger than others, but it's now known that—within very broad limits—brain size, determined by heredity, has nothing to do with intelligence. Others decided, largely on the basis of psychological tests, that some races or cultural groups were smarter than others, but it soon became obvious that the tests were faulty.

At the other extreme, some people have insisted that heredity has nothing to do with intelligence, but that at birth the brain was a blank slate, on which environment and experience created smarts and personality. However, research results disagree with that viewpoint. For instance, studies of identical twins and triplets (people whose genes are alike because they developed from the same two cells) raised in different families and cultures show great similarities in their skills and intelligence levels, indicating that heredity plays some role. Children who are adopted will take on many characteristics and interests of their adoptive parents, but will also be like their birth parents in many ways.

Since brain scientists are now fairly certain that every new experience permanently alters the brain, it's likely that the brain you inherited from your parents is not exactly the same as the one you will grow up with. What's inside your head is partly what you started out with, and partly what you've worked at.

How much of your intelligence and talents are due to heredity, and how much to environment—the world around you? Research hasn't yet broken it down accurately, but an old rule of thumb still seems useful: Heredity sets the limits on what you can learn and do, and environment determines how far and in which direction within those limits you will develop.

In any case, it's clear that both heredity and environment combine to outline how smart you are and in what ways.

...And After

The environment within which you—and your brain—grow and develop includes the physical setting and the opportunities within it for learning and experience, as well as the people who surround you.

Your family is, of course, a large part of that environment. If your parents enjoy reading, for instance, you are likely to imitate them, and that will set one direction for your development. (Or you might refuse to imitate them, which will set another direction.) It's likely that Sally's parents deal well with people, for instance, and openly or subtly have taught her to do the same. Phyllis the swimmer undoubtedly comes from a family that actively pursues sports: They not only gave her chances when she was young to develop her physical skills, but they also reward her efforts and give her support.

Your larger environment influences the way in which you develop your mind and skills. If you go to school with a lot of sports nuts, you are more likely to develop your body smarts than your book-learning skills. If your classmates think sports are silly, you may well ignore those talents in favor of more traditional schoolwork. These are examples, in a broad sense, of goal-directed adaptive behavior: We develop our intelligence in ways that will achieve goals that are, in part, influenced by those around us.

Different cultures value different forms of intelligence. In some parts of the world, people who can meditate themselves into tranquillity are considered wise, and others will strive to gain control of their minds' functions in the same way. In other places, it's the visibly successful people who are called smart, so members of those cultures are likely to work at developing the more active, verbal control centers of their brains.

In quite specific ways, too, your environment can influence your "cognitive style," or the way you use your head. If you are told, over and over, that you're a rotten student, you aren't likely to put much energy into developing the kind of intelligence that leads to success in school. Or, if you are praised often for your artistic skill or your athletic ability, you will probably work harder to develop those kinds of "smarts."

How You Make Connections

Why do you know what you know? You have learned it. That learning takes place in your brain, when an axon and a dendrite form a new link across a synapse. That learning also takes place within your environment, when what you perceive, feel, and do stimulates those brain cells to connect.

We learn best about what we can experience. You might read about llamas in a book, so that you would store in your brain some idea of what those South American animals look, feel, and even smell like. If you've seen llamas in a zoo, you have a clearer image of their characteristics in your mind. But if you lived among herds of them in the Andes mountains, you would have brain cells packed with information about how they live and behave. In the same way, a boy who has grown up with no music in his surroundings will likely not be musical; if a girl lives where only English is spoken, she will have to work harder at learning Spanish than one who hears it frequently.

We also learn best what we actively try to learn, and we need motivation to move us to try. We are best motivated to learn those things that bring a reward. For a rat lost in a laboratory maze, the reward is the food at the end and the electric shocks to avoid at the wrong turnings: It doesn't take long for a rat to lock the pattern of the maze into its brain cells. A South American teenager who gets paid or fed for watching a herd of llamas is motivated to learn as much as possible about those llamas. A child who is rewarded with praise for practicing a musical instrument well enough to store the fingerings in his brain will continue to practice and learn.

Learning requires the opportunity to perceive the necessary information, the ability to understand and code what is wanted, the brain cells to process the information, and the reward for storing the new learning in the brain.

Heredity, in the form of the patterns in your brain cells, and environment, in the form of the people and experiences you live with, are constantly interacting as you learn.

Both heredity and environment, for instance, influence our learning styles: Someone who inherits strengths in physical dexterity, say, and who grows up in a family of active people is more likely to need to learn by *doing* than someone whose genes have allowed for special verbal skills and who grows up in a family prone more to reading and talking than to physical activity. (You can find out more about *your* learning styles in Chapters 6 and 7.)

Since each of us has a unique heredity and an environment of experiences unlike that of anyone else, it should be obvious that there are almost infinite ways of being smart.

There are some ways in which heredity and environment only *seem* to influence intelligence. When people of different races (determined by heredity) and cultures (determined by environment) did poorly on intelligence tests, some researchers concluded that this indicated lower levels of intelligence among those races or cultures. A new look at the facts, however, has shown that those conclusions are false—that it is a case of the tests not measuring correctly, rather than of the test-takers not measuring up. For one thing, race and culture are often combined. An Indian (that's race) boy in a South American herding society (that's culture) wouldn't know what to make of a paper-and-pencil test that a white, English-speaking, middle-class boy takes as a matter of course. If the right kinds of tests could be designed to fit the needs and differences of every culture, race, and race-culture combination in the world, it is likely that they would reveal the same spectrum of intelligence levels within all of them.

Two factors, though—one inherited and one environmental—do have big effects on how all of us use
our heads. The common hereditary factor is sex, and
the environmental one we share is nutrition.

Sex Links

Heredity—the codes within the genes you inherit
from your parents—determines whether you are
male or female, and male and female brains are different. Neither is better than the other, but they are
different.

The average female brain is slightly smaller in size
and weight than that of the average male. Once it was
thought that the difference meant that men were
smarter than women. Now we know that brain size
simply reflects body size, and most women are
smaller than most men.

But, as current research is discovering, subtle and
probably significant differences exist within that
smaller brain. Females, for instance, have denser connections between the two halves of the cortex, which
may mean that they are better able than males to
focus all sections of the brain on a task. They also
seem to have learning and sensory centers scattered
more equally throughout the brain than men, whose
brains appear to be more rigidly organized. Perhaps
because of this difference, males in general are better
able to focus specific powers on problems to be

solved, while females tend to approach a problem from several different angles.

The organization of male brains seems to make them more adept at handling concepts of spatial relationships, for instance, while females are usually better at controlling the small, fine muscles required by precision work. Why these and other differences exist is not yet clear. Some researchers point to the fact that girls begin—and stop—developing physically at an earlier age than boys, so that the brain centers may not have time to differentiate as clearly as in boys. Hormones probably influence brain development and activity as well, and those body chemicals are quite different in boys and in girls. The testosterone that produces the male physical characteristics is unlike the estrogen that triggers the development of the female's, and it may be that those hormones influence the activity and shape of the brain. Much more investigation will be needed before these differences are fully understood.

Of course, the fact that their brains seem to be different does not mean that boys and girls can't be smart in the same ways. It just means that there may be inborn strengths and weaknesses to develop or overcome. After all, many men are creative artists, and many women are scientists and mathematicians —but it may be that each of them has to approach those "male" or "female" skills from different points.

Sex may be hereditary, but in today's environment,

there should be no limitation on learning because anyone is considered the "wrong sex" to work toward a given goal.

Brain Food

One ingredient for good brain development and function, over which we do have great control, is the food we eat. Balanced nutrition during pregnancy and early childhood produces not only strong bones, but strong minds as well, because it provides the nourishment that allows brain cells to multiply and form healthy patterns. It's been shown, too, that chemicals other than those found in foods can influence development: A pregnant woman who smokes, drinks alcohol, or uses other drugs can harm her baby's developing brain, as those chemicals pass from her bloodstream into the baby's.

But after birth, and in even more specific ways, foods can influence how well your head works. Foods are chemicals. The brain uses chemicals to transmit nerve signals, and the body turns food chemicals into transmitting chemicals that travel through the bloodstream to the brain. The brain cells won't accept every kind of chemical: They set up a barrier to protect themselves from some of the ones that will harm them or that they can't use, so it's important to provide the body with a variety of "brain foods." Tryptophan, one of the most vital transmitting chemicals, for instance, is derived from protein, but the brain can't make good use of it unless chemicals found in carbohydrates are also in the bloodstream. Tests have shown that another protein-based chemical, norepinephrine, affects the brain's emotional centers and can help alleviate depression.

Realizing the impact of food chemicals on the brain, doctors are working to find ways in which to use foods to help the brain work better and to cure some of the problems usually considered mental or psychological illnesses.

Some of the substances we take in can limit brain function and wreak havoc on our emotions. Alcohol, for instance, is one potentially harmful chemical that is able to penetrate the brain-cell barrier. It dulls judgment, motor control, and problem-solving ability. Other drugs—artificial chemicals—prevent the brain from producing its own transmitting substances, so that perceptions and moods are distorted. Obviously, the more you avoid those kinds of chemicals, the better your brain will work: That's another aspect of our environment that we do have control over.

In some people, heredity influences the brain's reactions to chemicals found in normal food. People who are sensitive or allergic to certain foods sometimes suffer reactions in their brains, just as they might break out in an allergic skin rash. As more becomes known about such "brain allergies," doctors are testing people who appear to have mental illnesses or learning disabilities, to see if what they eat is reacting with the brain's inborn chemistry system to affect the way they think and behave.

For most people, though, "feeding the brain properly" is simply a matter of eating a well-balanced diet, in order to take in the most useful combinations of chemicals.

More Questions

How smart you are and how you are smart involve a delicate balance, too: of heredity and environment; of what you have and what you can do with it. Those balances make for all the differences between people's personalities, talents, and skills.

What are some of the factors that influence the way you use your head?

What have you inherited in the way of motor ability, reasoning power, artistic talent, language skill?

What has your environment taught you about what you can, can't, should, or shouldn't do with those strengths and weaknesses?

In how many ways could you be smart?

(5)

The Different Ways of Being Smart

Book smarts, art smarts, body smarts, street smarts, and people smarts: These are the labels used in this book to describe the various forms of intelligence and their use. As you might imagine, psychologists and other researchers into the nature of intelligence have come up with more formal terms for the types that they have isolated. One set of labels in common use is: convergent, divergent, assimilating, and accommodating. The converger and assimilator are like our book-smart person; the diverger, like our art-smart; and the accommodator, like our street-smart and people-smart.

Whatever categorization we use, we will find some overlap within any individual. In fact, there are probably as many answers to the question: "What are the different ways of being smart?" as there are people in the universe, because each of us is unique. We can't be typecast; we each have a wide spectrum of special talents.

Still, you probably know well at least one person

whose talents generally fall into each of our categories. Keep those people in mind as you read through the detailed descriptions of them in this chapter.

At first, it might seem that each of those types must call on very different sorts of abilities to be smart in his or her own ways. But in fact, each of the categories of intelligence on our list must use the same ingredients discussed in Chapter 3: learning ability, memory, speed, judgment, problem-solving skill, good use of language and other symbols, and creativity. Also, the thought processes that go on inside the heads of people with those varying kinds of smarts include the same steps: planning, perceiving, imaging, remembering, feeling, and acting.

Intelligence expresses itself in different forms, in part because of the differing physical qualities born and built into each person's body and brain, and in part because of the values and motivations that each person has learned.

However, the fact that each kind of smarts makes use of the same steps means that anyone can learn or develop skills in any or all of the categories. Before we offer specific suggestions on how to go about this, let's take a closer look at the many ways of being smart.

Comparisons and Contrasts

A *book-smart* person is one who tends to do well

in school, to score high on tests, including intelligence tests. He or she is likely to be well organized, to go about solving problems in a logical, step-by-step fashion, and to have a highly developed language ability. Another label for a book-smart person is "intellectual," meaning someone who uses the mind more to *know* than to feel or to control, and a book-smart person is especially proud of having knowledge. That knowledge may range from literature through science to math, but it is probable that it is concentrated in one area. Research shows that different knowledge areas occupy different clusters in the brain, so that someone whose connections for complicated calculations are highly developed may have less development in the areas controlling speech and writing.

Although, as we've said, current brain research indicates that learning centers may be scattered throughout both hemispheres of the brain, the activities of the "logical" left side are probably most important in the lives of book-smart people. Book-smart people may also be quite creative: Many mathematical or scientific problems could not be solved, for instance, without creative insights, but the primary focus of a book-smart person is the increase of knowledge.

Art-smart people, on the other hand, rely primarily on creativity. They create music, paintings, sculpture, plays, photographs, or other forms of art often without being able to explain why or how they chose a particular form or design. They are said to be "right-brained" people, because it appears that the control centers for such skills as touch perception and intuition—the formation of ideas without the use of words—lie in the right hemisphere. Artistic people tend to take in knowledge more often by seeing, hearing, and feeling than by conscientious reading and memorizing.

An art-smart person may not do too well in school, not because he or she is not bright, but because of an approach to problem solving that does not fit in well with the formats usually used by teachers and tests. A book-smart person might approach a problem on a math test logically, working step-by-step toward the right answer, while an art-smart person may simply "know" the answer without being able to demonstrate the calculations involved. On a social studies exam, the book-smart person will carefully recount all the facts, while the more artistic one may weave stories and fantasies using the facts only as a base. In both cases, it's a good bet that the book-smart student will get the higher grade.

People who are serious about becoming artists, of course, may need to absorb a great deal of "book knowledge" in order to develop a solid background for their skills. There are other overlaps, as well: People with great musical ability, for instance, also tend to be skilled at mathematics, perhaps because of brain-cell interactions that are common to both processes. And in order to make use of any talent, art-smart people must have good body control as well.

The people we're calling *body smart* have a lot of that kind of body control. Most of them start out with bodies that are well put together for some kind of athletics—they may have inherited good muscular development for a sport like football, or loose and limber joints for gymnastic-style athletics. Or they may be people whose hands are naturally well coordinated for performing intricate tasks.

But although the physical basis for their talent may come from their genes and from especially sensitive brain centers for motor control, to make use of their "natural" skills they must bring higher levels of brain function into action. They must be able to observe accurately—to figure out how a move is made or an object is constructed—and they must think about how to do it themselves. This thinking involves a complex use of symbols that enables the brain to "tell" another part of itself what to do. In other situations, such as school, a body-smart person is probably best able to learn through some physical technique: In studying for an exam, for instance, he or she will retain information by saying it out loud, acting out the facts, or counting them off with finger taps. Although athletes or the manually talented are often teased as being "dumb" in schoolwork, that is not necessarily an accurate picture. To be good in using physical talents, a person must put in a lot of practice, be able to concentrate intently, and be stubbornly persistent in achieving a goal. And those qualities of will and self-control can also be put to good use in more "intellectual" achievements.

Persistence is also an important quality of *street-smart* people. They are the ones who are able to see difficulties as challenges, to turn almost any situation to advantage for themselves. As young people, they are the ones who are able to make the most money doing odd jobs, or who can get free tickets to a concert that others believe is completely sold out. As adults, they are the business tycoons, for instance, or the personalities who shoot to stardom no matter how much or little talent they have. A street-smart student may do well in the school subjects that he or she knows count for the most and will all but ignore the rest. When taking exams, street-smart people are likely to get better grades than their knowledge merits because they can "psych out" the test, and because, when facing a problem or question they can't answer, they are skilled at putting on the paper something that looks good.

To be street smart in these ways—to be able to achieve highly individualistic goals and to be able to get around obstacles that totally stump others—a person must draw on a wide scope of mental powers.

It takes excellent problem-solving ability, creative thought, good planning and goal setting, accurate perception, persistent effort, skill with language, quick thinking, and a strong sense of intuition.

Intuition plays a major role in *people smarts* as well. This kind of intelligence allows a person to sense what others are thinking, feeling, wanting, and planning. Although we might tend to put this sort of skill down as basic "instinct," it actually relies on higher activities of the brain. People smarts rely on very accurate and quick perceptions of clues and relationships that escape the notice of many, and they include the ability to analyze the information taken in. A people-smart student can do well in school simply by dealing with individual teachers in the most productive way: Some can be charmed, some respond well to special requests for help, some reward hard work no matter what the results, and so forth. The people-smart student figures out easily what is the best approach to take. People with these talents also achieve well in other activities, of course—they become the leaders in clubs and organizations, and they are able to win important individuals, like potential employers, over to their side. They would probably be typed as right-brained people, like artists, but their skill with language, both spoken and unspoken, is one that draws heavily on the left side.

Have you been able to compare these types with people you know in your class, family, or neighborhood? Of course, no individual is actually a type: People with any one of the kind of smarts that we've described also have some of the others. Skill in using one part of the brain does not mean that the other parts stay lazy. (There are people whom psychologists call *idiots savants,* or wise idiots, who have remarkable talents in one narrow area of mental ability, although they are severely retarded otherwise—but those cases are rare.)

Rather, some people are able to develop one set of brain-powered skills to a higher degree than others who are able to strengthen other talents.

One person's choice of which skills to develop results from the rewards that he or she receives from the family and the larger environment, but that choice is only one part of a larger picture, as we shall see when we look at the breadth of talents that each of our examples brings to his or her specialty.

A Few Examples

Jennifer is a book-smart person. In someone like her, the elements of intelligence that we've listed are especially obvious on her tests. She has good learning ability, which is aided by speed and a well-trained memory for facts. She uses judgment in deciding what facts to study for a test and which to include in her answers. She uses language well, both in interpreting the questions and in writing the answers. But what about creativity? Isn't she just a plodder? She certainly is careful and methodical, but she does bring creativity into play in her process for solving problems. On any good exam, the questions or problems are not exactly the same as the ones you've done for homework. So when Jennifer faces a math problem that's in a familiar form but calls for different figures, she must mentally take a variety of elements and put them together to create something new. That's creativity in the same valid sense as in finding an unfamiliar bus stop.

She brings creativity to the steps in her thought process when, say, she meets an essay question that calls for information contained in many chapters of a textbook plus some of the outside reading assignments for her course. She mentally plans what she must do, perceives the problem and all its parts, draws on her memory of what she's studied while forming images of what she's learned, and then, motivated by her desire to do well on the test, she acts: She writes an answer that has created something new from a variety of existing materials.

Alex the artist is easy to call "creative." But is he using his mind or some kind of gut instinct? Art smarts call for just as much intelligence as the more familiar kinds. As an example, let's see how he goes about solving a problem. The problem is how to create an image of his family that shows not just what they look like but what they *are* like, individually and as a group. He could make a photograph or paint a portrait, but that's too ordinary: He rejects those alternatives and continues to "turn the problem over in his mind"—he has put his brain into a mode similar to, but more complicated than, a computer's "search" for data. While he is going about his business, part of his brain is working on that problem, considering alternatives, such as a clay sculpture—but Alex doesn't feel he can sculpt well enough in enough detail, so he sets his brain searching again. And then, suddenly, it seems, he has it: He will make a tightly molded and unified figure, using different clays and different textures for each of the individuals that make up his family group. Although it would seem that the idea came to him in a "flash of inspiration," it actually took a lot of thought and mental action. He carries through on his problem-solving process as he selects materials and tools, decides on a size for his piece, makes judgments about its exact form, and carries through his plan, step by step.

Is *Phyllis*, our swimmer, just a jock? Sure, she works hard and manages to do all right in school despite her training schedule, and we can call her overall behavior intelligent, since it is "goal directed" (her goal is the Olympics) and "adaptive" (she is able to adapt herself to that goal). But does it take any brains to swim well? Is there such a thing as body smarts? Let's see how she goes about learning something as apparently minor as smoothing out her racing dive. If she can get it just right, she can take crucial seconds off her time in the crawl. Her coach tells her that her crouch is not deep enough, that she is arching her back a slight bit too far after she pushes off. He shows her what he means. She observes, then does it her own way, having her brain monitor the feelings in her muscles and joints as she does. *Ah,* she says to herself in the instant before she hits the water, *my back feels too tight.* She has produced a mental symbol for the information her coach demonstrated, and as she tries the dive again and again, she continues to use mental symbols to guide the process of making the correct brain connections for the perfect dive. "Perfect!" her coach says, and at that point, she locks into her brain the physical feeling that she had when she made the right moves. She will practice and practice so that her brain will retain the memory of those moves to use during the upcoming races. The perfect dive was no instinctive act: It took thought and intelligence.

Jason is an example of what we've called street smart. In sixth grade, he made enough money on his own to buy a stereo and a video game set. You might say that such success just took luck and energy, but it took intelligence and problem-solving skill as well. Let's examine just one of his transactions to show that. Keeping in mind his overall goal of making enough money for a fairly nice stereo, Jason has gone around his neighborhood, hustling up such standard odd jobs as lawn care and dog walking. One neighbor is constantly apologizing for the state of her garage, where Jason always has trouble storing the lawn mower among piles of cartons and old furniture. Every week, she says, "I must get rid of some of this stuff!" Those facts are stored in Jason's memory. One week, he is returning a dog to another neighbor, who says, "I wish I could find a place to put away all this extra china I got from my grandmother." Jason remembers the stuffed garage.

He goes back to the first neighbor and, using his intuition about people and his language skill, offers in just the right way to clean out her garage, for a fee. She agrees, and he returns to the lady with the china: "I've found a china cupboard for you, which you could have for free if you would use your station wagon to haul away some other stuff." He has used creativity to produce a new situation from old facts, and he has solved the problem of how to deal with the garage full of stuff. The next Saturday, he sweats his way through the garage and sorts things into different piles for the owner to examine, since his judgment is good enough that he knows he mustn't take every-thing, not only because that wouldn't be right or fair, but also because a bad reaction from the owner would get him into trouble. She takes what she wants and pays him for his work. The other neighbor hauls away the rest, pays Jason a tip for his help, and buys two more items from him. Jason convinces others to buy most of the rest, and he turns the dregs over to a junkyard for a small fee. He still has some old books left, so he donates them to a local community center, where his charm makes such an impression that the directors hire him to work in an afternoon program for preschoolers.

Each one of those steps, which brought him much closer to his goal, took planning, perception, imaging, memory, feeling, and action: in other words, in addition to some luck and energy, a lot of thought. Yet Jason is the despair of his parents, because he is doing poorly in school!

Sally has even more people smarts than Jason, and while he uses his as only a small part of his wheeling and dealing, in different ways they both have developed those skills to a high degree. People smarts are, like art smarts or body smarts, a talent that many regard as simply natural or instinctive. But they, too, require intelligence.

For instance, how did Sally learn to smile at the teacher in just the right way? When she was very young, she, like everyone else, wanted and needed to get just the right kind of attention from her parents. Of all the techniques she tried at random on her mother, a certain kind of look and tone of voice got the desired results. That success, like Phyllis's coach saying "perfect," locked the information into her memory. Trying the same approach on her father, she found it didn't work, so she had to adapt, and in that process, she learned that people were different. From that knowledge, connected up in her sensitive "intuition" centers, she conceived the idea that different people could be won over to her side in different ways. As she grew, her perceptions and observations became sharper, and she was able to practice more subtle processes on other people, drawing on her memories and images, until her skill, learned through a complex series of processes, now seems automatic. She has learned to respond to the teachers in a way not much unlike the way Jennifer has learned to find the right answers on an exam.

Each of those people, just like you, just like each of the people that you know, has chosen to develop intelligence in a different way, though each could apply the process to another area. Why? Remember Andrea, who hates school but organizes the musical to the last detail? She is using all kinds of smarts: book smarts, to find the script and get the rights to it; art smarts, to help design the sets; body smarts, to train the dancers; street smarts, to get the props and financial support she needs; and people smarts, to get the best out of her cast and staff. Yet she can't or won't draw on any of these areas of intelligence to make an effort in school. That's because she is not motivated to do well in school. In Andrea's case, she lacks motivation—the push to use her intelligence and thought processes—because she has two parents and five older brothers and sisters who all did well in school, and Andrea is determined to be different.

Kim could not be called book smart, but he had the motivation to learn English so that he could fit in with his new home. Steve might not realize that his memory and his persistence could be used to advance toward a goal; all he knows is that he loves baseball —he is motivated to learn all he can about it.

Each of us has our own motivations to use our brains in different ways.

(6)

How Are You Smart?

Your responses to the quizzes, questions, and exercises in this section will give you an idea of how *you* best use your head.

Are you smart with books, in art, with your body, with people, or "on the street"?

Are you a diverger, a converger, an assimilator, or an accommodator? Right brained or left brained?

What is your learning style? What motivates you to excel in one area or another?

How is your speed, memory, judgment, problem-solving ability, skill with symbols, creativity?

What is your image of yourself and your talents—and how does that image compare with the profile outlined by your responses in this chapter?

Although that profile is not likely to be as detailed or as psychologically precise as one derived from a formal battery of personality, aptitude, and intelligence tests, these informal questionnaires will give you some new insights into the ways in which you are smart. (For advice on finding sources for those, see pages 125–129.)

Test Yourself

Questionnaire Instructions: Please get a pencil and a pad of paper to work through these items. That way, you won't have to write in this book (which could cause trouble if the book isn't yours), and some of the responses may take more space than the book page allows. With your responses and a note of what they mean on separate paper, you'll have them handy as you read the rest of the book, and you may want to save them for comparison if you redo the questionnaire at some later date. Also, you should use the paper to cover up the analyses that accompany each section, so that you are sure to give the answers you want, and not the ones you think you "should."

Remember: There are no "right" answers to any of these questions. Just respond in the way that seems best to you and compare your responses with the comments following each section, making a note of what they indicate about you.

I. PERSONAL PROFILE

Think about these questions and jot the answers on a separate piece of paper.

1. In the past year, the achievement I've been

proudest of is: _____. Why?

2. In the past year, I have been most ashamed of: _____. Why?

3. The situation that frightens me the most is: _____. Why?

4. An activity I find most exciting is: _____. Why?

5. An activity I find most boring is: _____. Why?

6. In three of my friends, the quality I admire most is: _____. Why?

7. In three of my friends, the quality I envy most is: _____. Why?

8. In three of my friends, the quality I dislike most is: _____. Why?

9. You are the guest of honor at an awards presentation dinner. The person introducing you has a list of your outstanding characteristics and wants to present you to the audience in the best possible light. What is on that list?

10. And, by the way, at your imaginary awards dinner, what did you win an award for? Jot that down, too.

I. COMMENTS

Your answers to these questions are yours alone, but they should give you an idea of how you feel most comfortable in "using your head," whether for book learning, artistic pursuits, using your body, dealing with people, setting and meeting personal challenges, or some combination of those strengths. For instance, if your answer to item 3 is something like "having to think on my feet," you are probably not what we've called a street-smart person. Or, if your answer to item 1 is something you have made or built, you may feel best when using your body—your hands rather than your head.

Read through your answers carefully: Try to read them as though you were a stranger looking at someone else's profile. Do you find any surprises? If you've always thought of yourself as book smart, for instance, but read that you find an athletic event "most exciting," then you might think about taking a break from the books sometimes and getting involved in sports. Even if you didn't find surprises—if you'd always known that you were an art-smart person, for example—this profile can help to confirm your image of yourself and perhaps start you thinking about more ways to develop your talents.

In any case, save your answers, both for future reminders of your particular strengths and for a comparison right now with the next sets of questions.

II. WHAT KIND OF SMART ARE YOU?

You may not like *any* of the activities in these questions, but within each group, pick the *one* that you would like the most and note it on your pad of paper.

1. In my free time, I would most like to:
   a. listen to music by myself
   b. play music by myself
   c. dance to music
   d. go to a concert with friends
   e. organize a concert
2. I would rather:
   a. watch sports on TV
   b. report on or photograph a game
   c. play in an athletic game
   d. go to a game with friends
   e. manage a team
3. When I have "nothing else to do," I:
   a. read a book
   b. listen to music
   c. build or make something
   d. hang out with friends
   e. gather people for a card game
4. I would spend extra money on:
   a. a book
   b. hobby supplies
   c. exercise equipment
   d. a gift for someone
   e. a lottery ticket
5. The game closest to the kind I most enjoy is:
   a. video
   b. fantasy adventure

c. basketball
d. any board game
e. poker

II. COMMENTS

In the items above, the more often you answered *a*, the more book smart you are likely to be. A lot of *b* responses are a sign of art smarts. More *c* answers than others show body smarts. If you responded often with *d*, you tend to be people smart. And the *e* responses indicate street smarts. (But note that even though you were to pick only one item in each section, there were probably others that were close calls. Most people have talents and interests in more than one area.)

III. RIGHT BRAIN OR LEFT BRAIN?

Note the answers to these on another sheet of paper.
1. When I need to come up with an idea or the solution for a problem, I:
   a. analyze and research carefully, and persist until I succeed
   b. wait until an inspiration hits me
2. The papers that I turn in at school:
   a. get good grades because they always follow a pattern (mine, the teacher's or someone else's) that has succeeded in the past
   b. don't always get as good grades as other people's, but are almost always unique

3. Finish these phrases with a few words:
   A flower is . · . .
   Night is like   .
   In the ocean on a cold, gray dawn, I see . . . .
   Fire is . . . .
   My heart is like . . . .
4. When I am preparing to work on a project or
   take a trip, I: ·
   a. plan carefully, make lists and arrangements,
      gather ahead of time what I will need
   b. "wing it" and take care of needs as they arise
5. When I outline class notes or material for a
   paper, it tends to look like this:
   a. I. _____
          a. _____
          b. _____
      II. _____
          a. _____
          b. _____
   b.

or

6. If I had to choose a game to play, I would pick:
   a. chess
   b. charades
7. When I'm out with friends, I get annoyed and impatient:
   a. when people spend a lot of time and talk trying to decide what to do
   b. when people try to schedule the time and activities down to the last detail
8. If I had to choose, I would prefer to:
   a. visit an art museum
   b. paint a picture

III. COMMENTS

On all but item 3, the more *a* responses you gave, the more likely are you to be a left-brained person—one whose strengths lie in logical, step-by-step thinking. A majority of *b* responses indicate a probable right-brain dominance, relying more on unstructured creativity and intuition.

Now, think about item 3. Did you finish the first phrase with something factual like: " . . . the blossom of a plant, produced as part of the regeneration system"? That's left brained, as is any accurate, matter-of-fact completion of that phrase or the others. Or did you respond on the order of: "A flower is the soul's most happy sigh"? The more poetic, fantastic, or "unrealistic" your reactions to the phrases, the more right brained you tend to be.

Though, as noted previously, these divisions are not absolute, for either people in general or individuals in particular, they can serve as guides for finding comfortable ways to achieve your goals.

IV. WHAT KIND OF LEARNER ARE YOU?

Note on your paper the best answer to each question.

1. When I study for an exam, I prefer to work:
   a. by myself
   b. with one other person
   c. with a group of people
   d. with an adult's help
2. I need to move around a lot when I study.
   a. true
   b. false
3. I concentrate best when I can eat, drink, suck, or chew on something.
   a. true
   b. false
4. I am most alert in the:
   a. morning
   b. afternoon
   c. evening
   d. late evening and night
5. I remember best those things which I:
   a. see
   b. hear
   c. touch
   d. experience

6. I work most comfortably:
   a. sitting at a desk
   b. lying down
   c. slouching in a chair
   d. standing up
7. I feel most comfortable when the . . .
   . . . lights are: (a) bright; (b) dim
   . . . temperature is: (a) cool; (b) warm
   . . . space is: (a) quiet; (b) noisy
8. I tend to finish a project:
   a. at the last minute
   b. a little at a time
   c. only when I'm reminded
   d. only when I want to
9. When I'm involved in a project, I'm happiest:
   a. working alone
   b. working with a partner
   c. working with a team
   d. working under adult supervision
10. In any of my favorite activities, I do best when I:
    a. can compete
    b. can cooperate
    c. can take credit for myself
    d. receive praise from my friends
11. When I want some extra money, I:
    a. ask my parents
    b. ask my friends
    c. find some work

    d. wait till the next allowance day
12. To learn a new song, I would need to:
    a. read the sheet music
    b. listen to it several times
    c. play it on an instrument
    d. tape it, then repeat it phrase by phrase
13. The teacher I like best:
    a. tells me what to do to get a good grade
    b. makes class dramatic
    c. listens to what I have to ask
    d. suggests projects
14. If I wanted to bake a cake, I would:
    a. read the recipe that sounded best
    b. watch someone else do it, then try
    c. use a mix
    d. ask someone to show me

IV. COMMENTS

Each of us learns—and thinks—best within a particular set of situations made up of a variety of factors. These factors are *physical:* what we do with our bodies (and when) as we learn, study, or think; *environmental:* what we like surrounding us; *sociological:* whom we like to work with; and *emotional:* what triggers our learning process. For some people, these factors are of more importance than they are to others, but they all influence the mind's activity to some extent.

Your responses to items 2, 3, 4, 5, 12, and 14

outline the physical aspects of your learning style. Items 2, 3, and 4 give you important clues about the best ways to "bribe" your mind into thinking and the best time to do it. Five, 12, and 14 show you which of your senses most efficiently convey information to your particular brain.

Items 6 and 7 relate to the best environment for your learning or thinking activity. The next time you are having trouble working out a problem, look around you: If you are not comfortable, do what you can to adjust the surroundings more to your liking.

Your responses to items 1, 9, 10, and 11 give you an idea of the type and number of people you prefer to work with or to ask for help. For both companionship and work, some people do best alone, some are more comfortable as part of a pair, some relate best to groups, and some turn to adults.

In order to learn or to solve problems, different people require different "emotional" triggers, and items 8 and 13 offer clues to whether you rely on inspiration, organization, persistent pressure, or a sense of responsibility.

Go back over your responses to get a clear idea of the circumstances under which your mind works best.

V. PROBLEM SOLVING

Note the best answers to these on your answer pad.

1. When I have to take an exam, I *mind least:*
   a. short-answer questions
   b. long essays
   c. surprise quizzes
   d. short essays
2. You are on a solo hike in the country and have gotten lost. From the top of a hill, in one direction, you can see a dirt road on the other side of some dense-looking woods; in the other directions, you see empty meadows. No houses or people are in sight. You have some food and water and a little bit of money. You have a map, but you don't know where to find your current location on it.

How would you get yourself out of this situation?
   a. I wouldn't—I would just enjoy the adventure and keep hiking.
   b. I would head through the woods to the road and wait for someone to come along.
   c. I would go to the woods and walk till I got to a house.
   d. I would avoid the woods and walk through the meadows until I found help.
   e. I would figure out my location by using my watch and the position of the sun, then use the map to find the nearest town.
   f. I wouldn't have gotten into the situation in the first place, because . . . .
   g. I would choose this other solution: _____.

V. COMMENTS

There are many approaches to problem solving. One set of descriptions of people who use these approaches includes convergers, divergers, assimilators, and accommodators (see pp. 55–69).

For example, if in item 1 you responded *a,* you are likely to be a converger, comfortable with cut-and-dried facts. Divergers—people good at turning concrete facts into new ideas through brainstorming—are likely to identify with *b.* Accommodators tend to be risk-takers, so they would feel safe with surprise quizzes, or *c.* Assimilators, who are good at organizing facts and concepts into tight packages, would probably respond with *d.*

For the situation described in item 2, did you pick the response or responses that offered the least risk (such as *d* or *e*) or the most (such as *a* or *b*)? In any of the possible solutions, including *f* or *g,* did you tend to rely on facts and planning as a book-smart, or perhaps left-brained, person would? Did you stake your confidence on your own physical skills, like a body-smart person? Or did you pick one that depended on people to help you? Think about your answers and imagine yourself into another similar situation, to give yourself a perspective on how you approach a problem or challenge, and whom or what you rely most on to resolve it.

VI. WHAT MOTIVATES YOU?

Think carefully about these questions before responding on your separate sheet.

1. When, while taking a test, I come up against a question or problem I just can't answer, I:
   a. skip it
   b. work at it until I come up with something
   c. ask for help from the teacher
   d. worry about it, because I know I have to do well
   e. do my best on the rest of the test, to make up the points

2. You are the manager of a plant whose employees have been on strike for a week because of complaints against the higher management of the company. What do you suggest for settling the strike?

3. In a class, Jane wants to do well because her parents demand it; Jeff wants to because he wants to get into an A-one college; Jerry wants to because he needs to make a good impression; Jackie, because she likes the course; and Jocelyn wants to do well because her friends do. Which student has the best reason? And the next? and so forth. . . . Which of the five is most like you? Why?

VI. COMMENTS

We learn, think, and work best when we are motivated to do so. Motivation can come from outside ourselves, from within us, or from a combination of sources. Your responses to these items give clues to your motivation.

For instance, on item 1, *a* can indicate low motivation. Response *b* may show a strong internal motivation stemming from persistence or stubbornness, which can be self-defeating if it interferes with doing well in other areas. The motivation behind response *c* may be a combination of external (from the teacher) and internal (from a desire to do well). The person responding *d* likely feels motivation in the form of pressure, whether externally from parents, teachers, friends, or internally from fear of failure. What response *e* shows most is internal motivation based on good self-discipline, perhaps combined with a desire to meet external goals.

If your suggestions for the situation in item 2 rely primarily on threats ("fire them all," "dock their pay," and so forth), you may tend to count on motivation from outside yourself. If they run along the lines of: "Explain to the workers the reasons for the situation," then you probably count on internal motivations. A response like: "Try to meet their demands, but only within certain limits" shows a combination of motives.

In item 3, Jane and Jocelyn are motivated by external situations; Jerry by a combination; and Jeff and Jackie largely by internal forces. Which are you most like?

VII. CREATIVITY

These responses may take up a lot of space on your answer sheet.

1. Describe all the things you could do or make with a wire clothes hanger.
2. Here are a few lines that will form the basis of any picture you want to make. Please copy them onto a piece of paper, so that you can work from them. You may take as long as you wish to make them into the picture of your choice on your own piece of paper, but pay attention to how long you spent in making your picture.

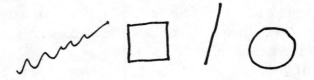

3. You are on a plane, sitting next to a man with an open briefcase. He suddenly glances toward the window and looks pale. Why?
4. Mark and Margery are found, dead, on the floor. Around them are a small puddle of water and bits of broken glass. You are responsible for finding out how they died. What do you figure out, and how?

VII. COMMENTS

The more flexible the patterns in your brain, the

more new ways you can find to use it. How flexible are yours?

Item 1: From hanging clothes, through roasting marshmallows, to making a wall sculpture: If you came up with twenty or more uses, your "creativity quotient" is high. For more practice, come up with as many uses as you can for a brick, a tennis ball, used tires, or one old sock.

Look again at the picture you made: How different is it from the lines you started out with? If you can barely find those original lines, you're quite creative; if the new pattern looks much like the original, you're probably a matter-of-fact person.

Does your response to item 3 consist of: "The engine is on fire"? Or is it more along the lines of: "A gigantic purple cloud is rushing toward the plane, and in it . . . ." The more fantastic and freewheeling your explanation, the more creative your imagination. To stretch your creativity, let your imagination run through the situation again and think of all possible—and impossible—explanations.

Item 4 shows how creativity and logical analysis can combine. Mark and Margery are goldfish whose bowl has fallen off the table. Logical analysis requires facts, but finding the facts in this case requires creativity.

VIII. STRENGTHS WITHIN YOUR INTELLIGENCE

A. For these items, you should get a timer, a clock,

or a watch with a second hand. Before you start reading the paragraphs below, note on a piece of paper your beginning time. When you've finished reading and noting your answers, you'll note the time, too.

1. Sandra sat in the Sahara because her jeep had broken down and her brother, Jeb, who was younger than she, had gone to find help. It was very hot, but she kept herself cool with the ice-packs that her mother, Rachel, had packed into their lunchbag. She and Jeb had gone into the desert to trace the findings that their father had made about the socioeconomic structure of the aboriginal Saharan people, but all that they had found was sand. She was beginning to worry, because night was not far off, and . . . .

2. Barnaby had gotten out of the yard because Priscilla had left the gate open, and now Priscilla's brother, Nicholas, had to find Barnaby. Barnaby wasn't anything fancy, but Nick had loved him ever since he'd found him hanging around lost in the park downtown. Priscilla and Nick's other sister thought Barnaby was a mess, and it was true that he was always causing trouble of one sort or another, but he was so friendly that you couldn't help loving him. As Nicholas searched, he only hoped that . . . .

Now, note your time, and without looking at the paragraphs again, answer these questions:

A-1. a. What was the mother's name?
  b. What had the two gone to look for?
  c. What had gone wrong?
  d. How old is Sandra?
  e. What was a better way to handle the situation?
  f. How will the story end?

A-2. a. What kind of creature is Barnaby?
  b. How many sisters does Nicholas have?
  c. What should Nicholas do first to find Barnaby?
  d. How was the gate opened?
  e. What did Nicholas "only hope" as he searched?

B-1. For these questions, set your timer and, as quickly as you can, jot your responses on a piece of scrap paper.
  a. List as many words as you can that mean the same thing as "bad."
  b. How many separate words of any length can you make from the letters of the word *caterpillar?*
  c. What should be the next letter in this series?
  A Z E Y I X O W __

d. List as many words as you can that mean the opposite of the word "together."

e. After intercepting a number of coded messages from an enemy spy, government agents had learned that QWERLYOP POTYUK meant "Beware Smith." They also learned that PO-TYUK BLIFNY meant "Smith Agent." How would that spy write in his code the message: "Beware Agent"?

Stop now, and note your time.

B-2. Set your timer again and answer the following problems as quickly as you can, without using a calculator.

a. What number is wrong in this sequence?
   3 2 9 4 27 6 81 10

b. Which combination of these numbers adds up to 325?
   42 50 100 38 73 101 22

c. When you multiply 73.45 by 100, you get:
   .7345 7,345 734.50 71,345

d. When you divide, multiply, add, or subtract these numbers:
   7 4 112 56 84
   how many times can you come up with this number? 28

e. Michael devised a number code to send secret messages to his friend George. He numbered the letters of the alphabet backward, so that A=26 and $Z=1$. This was the message that George got:

19 18 23 22 10 6 18 24 16

What does 10 6 18 24 16 mean?

Now, note your time for those questions.

VIII. COMMENTS

"Intelligence" is made up of problem-solving ability, creativity, memory, judgment, use of symbols, and speed.

Item A offers you a chance to check up on all of those factors. Here are the answers to the questions, and what they test:

A-1. a. Rachel (memory)
   b. To trace their father's research (memory and careful reading—use of symbols)
   c. The jeep had broken down (judgment shows that this is a better answer than "they found only sand")
   d. You don't know (memory—also, judgment and problem solving, which say that all you know is that she's older than her brother)
   e. That's your guess: The more imaginative the answer, the stronger your creativity.

A-2. a. You don't know (memory—though judgment tells you he's a dog, and creativity makes him anything at all)

b. Probably two (memory, use of word symbols, and problem solving)

c. Go to the downtown park (memory and problem solving)

d. Priscilla left it open (memory)

e. Your choice—factual or imaginative?

How long did you take to read the two paragraphs? Three minutes is a good time: The faster the time and the more correct answers, the speedier your mind.

Here are the answers to the B items—but it's not just the right answers that are important.

B-1. a. evil, wicked, rotten, nasty, poor, etc.—did you think of at least ten?

b. cat, pill, pillar, pile, pale, price, rice, race, rate, pare, pear, trap, trace, etc.—did you come up with at least twenty?

c. U (the next vowel)

d. apart, separate, split, detached, unconnected, etc.—did you come up with at least eight?

e. QWERLYOP BLIFNY

B-2. a. the last (it should be 8)

b. all of them but 101

c. 7,345

d. 7×4; $4 \div 112$; $84-56$; $4 \div 84 + 7$; $112 - 84$; did you think of any others?

e. "quick"

Now compare your time and the number of correct answers for both B-1 and B-2. If B-1 was much faster and better, you are more comfortable with word symbols; if B-2 was more successful, you deal better with number symbols. If both were about the same, you deal with symbols as symbols, because both sets of questions were essentially the same—they simply used different types of symbols. Many people's brains deal better with words than with numbers, and vice versa, but practice in the area where you are weaker can strengthen your abilities.

IX. SELF-DESCRIPTION
The responses to these may be important for you to save.

1. I would describe myself (using the descriptions in this book) as:
   a. book smart
   b. art smart
   c. body smart
   d. people smart
   e. street smart
   f. some of the above (which?)
   g. none of the above (why?)
2. Ask five other people (friends and/or family members):
   what you're best at doing
   what you're worst at doing
   . . . and ask them why they think that.

3. Compare the results of the above two items with each other and with your responses to the previous questions in this chapter.

IX. COMMENTS

If your own estimates of yourself came close to the judgments of your friends and family *and* came close to the profile created by your answers to the other questions in this chapter, you have a fairly clear idea of how you best "use your head." If your idea of yourself differs much from that of others or from the indications of your questionnaire responses, then you need to do some rethinking about what you *are* good at.

In either case, you will be smart to work at using your head in the best way for you.

(7)

Using <u>Your</u> Head

What did your answers to those questions show about you? Do you tend to be book smart, art smart, body smart, street smart, or people smart?

How close to your own judgment of your own skills and strengths did those answers come?

Whatever your answers, they should start you asking yourself some important questions that will, perhaps, turn your head toward new directions.

For instance: How would you *like* to be smart? How can you develop your own strengths to their best? How can you put the skills that you already have into the service of other achievements that you would like to add?

Unfortunately, many of us develop, sometimes very early in life, ideas about what we "can" and "can't" do or about what we "are" and "aren't." Those ideas can limit what we try. We are motivated to do the things for which we've been rewarded in some way in the past. Phyllis wouldn't be swimming if she hadn't received praise for doing well at it. Jennifer might be more active in sports if she had found some encouragement when she was younger. So Phyllis may think of herself as "just a jock," and Jennifer may consider herself "only an egghead," though they may have many other strengths to call on.

What about you? If the last chapter turned up any surprises about you yourself, that may be because you didn't think of your special skills and interests as being "smart." Most of us have an inner feeling about what it is we're good at, but we often see ourselves more clearly if we have a mirror—in the form of someone else's opinion or the results of some kind of test—through which to view ourselves.

Now, the trick is to make good use of what's inside your head. You can do that in two ways: to develop your kind of smarts as well as possible; and to use those same skills to strengthen areas where you are weak.

Accentuate the Positive

The most important thing you can do for yourself is to give yourself a lot of credit and a big pat on the back for all that you are good at. Too often, people think only about their weaknesses and not about their strengths.

Someone who is very bright, but who is surrounded by people who are just a little bit brighter, may think of himself as "dumb." A superb athlete who competes with people who have a slight edge on her may feel like a klutz.

So the first step toward making the best use of your head is to look a little more closely at those mirrors you've been reflecting in. Who is holding them, and from what angle?

Teachers, for instance, have an easier time dealing with students whose skills fit the mold of their systems and tests, so if you have unusual talents, or talents that lie outside the classroom, they may have caused you get a distorted idea of yourself. A family that has always been sports minded may make a bookworm feel silly, or one made up of solid business-people may make a talented actor feel like a failure. Or, if all your friends seem only to like having fun and getting by, you may feel like a fool if you take life seriously, and so forth. What really counts, though, is what you are good at, what skills make you—inside —feel good about yourself: That gives you the *motivation* for excellence.

Then, you need to find ways to *practice* those skills. Just as repeating a piano piece or a golf swing over and over locks it into the muscles and the brain's control centers, so finding as many ways as possible to exercise your particular brand of "smarts" will develop them to their peak.

People complain that schools don't provide opportunity for the development of a variety of talents.

Teachers encourage someone like Jennifer, but have trouble handling more creative or oddball types like artistic Alex or street-smart Jason. In some cases, that might be true, but even if it is, you can find many outlets for your talents that are outside the confines of the standard classroom walls.

Jason, for instance, might join Junior Achievement or other organizations where he could learn how to run a real business. He might take one of his many odd jobs and focus on it to develop a business of his own. He might lead charity drives that require his kind of hustle to get people to contribute food or money for a worthy cause, or volunteer to be in charge of getting prizes for the school fair. He should be thinking about what kind of schooling he is going to need to advance in the business career that seems so right for him, and there are afterschool and weekend courses that he could take now. Or he could ask local businesspeople to help him learn all about how their businesses are run.

Alex should be taking as many art courses, in and out of his regular school, as he can, and he should find out about special high schools, public and private, where he could go to develop his talents fully. He could volunteer to help younger kids learn and practice art at a day-care center or community playgroup. He should enter his art in as many exhibitions or contests as possible, and he might help organize exhibitions in his school or neighborhood, or serve as the art director for the yearbook. Whenever he can, he should visit museums and art galleries, and read and study art books, to learn how other artists have expressed themselves.

Activities like those not only provide ways to develop all the various kinds of smarts, but they also provide outlets for special skills that are rewarding in themselves. They build up a portfolio of achievement that will impress future employers or admissions officers. Remember—it's not just book smarts or high test scores that open doors for future opportunities.

In the meantime, what are you doing with your "smarts"?

To come up with ideas for making the most of your strengths, brainstorm or fantasize.

To brainstorm, concentrate intensely on one idea or goal, and open your mind (you should be able to feel your mind almost literally open up) to any thought, no matter how silly it seems, that occurs on that topic. It's quite an accurate description of what should happen inside your head, because as lightning flashes and rain pelts down during a thunderstorm, those electrochemical signals race through your brain, often making unexpected connections.

Or you may be the type of thinker who is more comfortable with fantasizing. Instead of forcing your mind to focus, let it wander where it will, always against the background of your desire to find outlets for your interests. Let your imagination take your thoughts anywhere they want to go, and see what ideas you bump into.

Try either brainstorming or fantasizing now. Have pencil and paper handy to note, shorthand style, any and all ideas you come up with for making creative and productive use of your "smarts."

How many ideas do you get? Some of them may seem farfetched, but none is likely to be impossible if, as the saying goes, you put your mind to it. Then, take some concrete steps to put those ideas into action.

Regroup

Of course, that might be the easy part—finding ways to exercise skills you already have. You also may want to learn new ways of "being smart."

Jennifer, for instance, might not like being viewed only as the smartest kid in the class. She may wish for the skill to get along better with people, so that she would have more fun and friends. Kim may want to improve not only his new language, but his old athletic skills, as well. Jason the hustler will do better for himself if he can focus more of his talents in the classroom, and so forth.

What are some of the things you wish you were

better at? That wish is the beginning of motivation—
and motivation is the first step toward learning a new
skill, whether it's in athletics, schoolwork, creative
art, or human relationships.

And before you say, "I can't," stop! Remember
that learning is simply the forging of links between
brain cells. Every time you try something new or
think a new thought, you begin to *learn* something
new. The more you work at it, the stronger you make
those brain connections and the better you will become. You would never get to the bus stop if you
never tried, and the more often you find your way to
new bus stops, the easier it gets.

Remember, too, that learning is problem solving,
and you already are good at problem solving in some
area of thought. All you need to do is to transfer that
skill to another area: to make an analogy—see a
similarity—between what you can do and what you
want to do. It's no accident that many of the items
on intelligence tests are analogies or comparisons,
such as, "Fence is to gate as _____ is to door,"
and the like, in words or pictures. Suppose that Andrea decides she wants to study better for tests because she's found out that the drama school she
wants to attend requires a high average (that's *motivation*). She realizes that studying is like putting on
a show: breaking the whole into manageable parts to
rehearse and then putting it all together again (that's

problem solving by analogy). She does it first for one course, and then for another and another, until all of her grades go up (that's *practice*).

A student who's good in math but terrible in grammar will do better if he or she realizes that grammatical rules are just like mathematical formulas, except that they use words instead of numbers.

Phyllis's athletic training has helped her learn to observe and have her brain make her body do what she has observed. In the same way, she can get over being shy with people by observing how outgoing people behave, and having her brain make her body do what they do.

Alex's skill at art shows that he is good at following through on a creative idea, so he might make some extra money by following through on an idea about how to sell some of his art.

Jennifer does well on school reports and tests, in part because she learns quickly and is well organized. If she wants to become more socially involved, in Andrea's style, she can apply those skills to club activities. If someone like Jason is getting into trouble in school (and may find motivation in the fear of being suspended), all he needs to do is concentrate on ways to bring the kind of discipline and charm into school that he uses to achieve success outside of it. If Kim applies the same kind of hard work and determination to learning a sport as he did to learning English, he can become skillful at it.

Problem solving involves perceiving the problem, mentally exploring ways to approach it, drawing on memories and mental images, making a plan, and choosing techniques to carry out the plan. Those steps apply to any situation, from working a math equation to running for president.

Try it yourself. Think of something you'd really like to do, but have never, or rarely, done. It might be painting a picture, starting a dogwalking business, making three new friends in a week—anything. Then go step by step: Decide what to do, figure out ways to go about it—drawing on any experiences you've ever had—plan your action, and carry out your plan.

Remember the definition of intelligence as goal-directed, adaptive behavior: When you set a goal for yourself and adapt your thoughts and actions toward reaching it, you are using your intelligence.

Stretch!

Whether your goal is to be a more book-, body-, people-, art-, or street-smart person, your adaptation process may need to include strengthening your skills in any or all of these areas of intelligence: problem solving, judgment, memory, use of symbols, speed, and creativity.

To get you started, here are some ideas for exercises that will help you extend your abilities.

PROBLEM SOLVING AND JUDGMENT

The two basic approaches to solving a problem —any problem—are through *logical analysis* (left brained) or through *intuitive insight* (right brained). Often, whether we realize it or not, we combine the two. Also, whether we realize it or not, whenever we solve any kind of problem we bring *judgment* into play, because most problems have several solutions, and we need to judge which is the most suitable.

The best way to become a good problem solver is to practice solving problems, so you'll need to dig up some that you can put your mind to, and luckily, the world does not lack for problems of all sorts. You can find them in your textbooks, probably at the end of every chapter. You can find them in the newspaper, in the advice columns, the feature stories, and the front-page news. You can find them in the plots of novels and mystery stories you read and in the television shows you watch. You can also find them, of course, in your own life and in the lives of your friends. So make a collection, right now, of problems to solve: think-questions from some texts, issues in the news, or situations from fiction or real life.

Now try to solve them. For some, use the "left-brained" approach: Organize into lists the pros, cons, and possibilities for every possible solution; or start with the basic facts and, mentally or with paper and pencil, go step by step from the facts to the logical consequences of each stage of the possible solution.

For others, use the intuitive approach: Solve the problem in your "gut," then see if it makes sense.

Here's an example: Forty percent of the freshman English class failed last semester's course. This is a larger number than ever. What should be done about it?

- "Logical" approach number 1:

  let them
  repeat   . . . but . . .   not fair?
  tutor them
  all   . . . but . . .   impractical.
  better
  preparation   . . . but . . .   too late now.
  adapt course . . . no "but" . . . best idea for
                                         now.

- "Logical" approach number 2:

  a. If students failed because they goofed off, then they should repeat, but if that is not the reason, then that solution is not fair, so
  b. Tutoring them might work if they need extra help. Then . . .

    . . . and so forth through each step of reasoning, until . . .

  (x). Whether the failures were due to student apathy, inadequate preparation, too-difficult work, poor teaching, or inaccurate testing, any of those problems can be solved by adapting the course for the second semester, a solution that is also practical and fair.

- The intuitive approach:
  "There's got to be something wrong with the course! Now, let's see what we can do about it."

Notice that all approaches came to the same conclusion, and all involved judgment. One solution might be: "Kick them all out of school"; another: "Fire the teacher!" But neither of those is suitable for the situation. Likewise, a conflict between a mother and daughter might be resolved if the girl told her mother to leave home—but your judgment would say that's not appropriate. Or on a math test, judgment will tell you that a problem is probably not "impossible," no matter how difficult it seems.

To combine approaches to any solution, a useful technique is to plot out all the logical steps, then tuck them away in the "back of your mind" to let your unconscious, intuitive processes come up with an answer. Or, "jump" to a conclusion, then outline the arguments for it logically.

Once you've worked through your collection of problems, you'll probably realize that you're better at problem solving than you thought. Then, try to do a few others every day: You'll find that it comes almost automatically, whether on math tests or in life crises.

In the meantime, make the most of what you have, while working to strengthen what you don't have: If you tend to be an intuitive person, go with that strength and work to back it up with step-by-step organization; if you tend to be logical and analytical, practice loosening up a little to let your unconscious insights come into play.

MEMORY

To remember something—anything—we need to get it from our short-term memories into our long-term memories (see pages 29–30). To make remembering useful, we need hooks or triggers to grab a memory back when necessary. When you are studying for an exam, you need to use whatever technique works best for you to lock facts into your memory— writing them down, saying them out loud, singing them, acting them out, rehearsing them with friends, or whatever your learning style makes most comfortable. Unfortunately, memory experts say, improving your overall memory ability is not simply a matter of using those techniques repeatedly until your memory becomes "muscle bound."

Rather, they recommend several processes that can get you into the habit of remembering anything easily. One is to use the substitution of simple ideas to recall more difficult ones. Another is to employ imagination to make associations with things you want to remember, and a third is to devise mental "hooks" onto which you "hang" facts to be remembered. On pages 125 to 128 you will find books that will help you learn these various memory tricks and techniques; if you want to stretch your memory, their exercises will prove more thorough than any we have space for here.

The good news about memory improvement is that it, too, requires that you make the best of what you have: Just as, when studying for exams, you will be most successful if you use your particular learning style to cram, so one among the possible systems will feel comfortable and easy for you, and that is the one that you should use.

USING SYMBOLS

For these purposes, "symbols" are words and numbers, and practice with these is easy. The more you read and write, for example, the more comfortable you'll feel using words, so if you make a habit of always having a fun-to-read book going and of keeping a diary, you'll be exercising your symbolic powers while enjoying yourself, too. And in your library or bookstore, you'll find lots of workbooks, often in the form of test-preparation guides, designed to increase your skill with language. It's not so much a matter of memorizing vocabulary as it is of working through practice exercises that will help you to understand the relationships between words and ideas. Word games, too, are both fun and useful: crossword puzzles, anagram-type games, and others played either with paper and pencil or with boards and cubes can build your confidence with these all-important symbols.

Some people have no trouble with words, but freeze up when faced with numbers. In part, this is because words and numbers are apparently handled by different parts of the brain—yet you can work to build up those connections, once you get over any fear of them. After all, numbers are symbols, just like words, and the more you practice with them, the more comfortable with them you will become. Work the "extra" problems at the back of each math chapter, for instance—not to turn in, but for your own purposes. Start the practice of keeping track of your personal budget and expenditures, which will get you used to having numbers run through your head and your pen or pencil—or keep records of the wins, losses, and other statistics for your favorite sport. Many games involve numbers, too—how many times have you played cards without realizing you were "doing math"? Now you have a good excuse to play cards! And you'll find many workbooks that will help you develop skills with numbers and number concepts. Again, you don't need to *memorize* math or formulas: The guides are meant to exercise your ability to manipulate nonverbal symbols.

Here, too, make the best use of what you have: If you tend to be better with words than with numbers —or vice versa—transfer your skills with one to your concerns with the other. Think of math as being "like grammar," for instance, or of grammar as being "like math."

CREATIVITY

Creativity is not just for artists—it is an important part of anything you do: Scientists are creative, as are mathematicians; auto mechanics require as much creativity as do cooks. Creativity is also something you can develop. In Chapter 6, you found questions like, "How many things can you do with a wire coat hanger?" The more games like that you do, the more elastic your creative power will become. Or, try the "What if . . ." game: Take any topic (from life, the paper, a story, your imagination) and ask "What if *x* happened instead of *y?*" Follow your train of thought wherever it leads. Some books listed on pages 125 to 128 offer good suggestions for other "games" like these, to shake loose some of the creativity that may be locked in your brain cells.

Find ways to express your creativity: You may protest that you aren't an artist, but you don't need to be. You can take photographs that are more than snapshots, create a picture with anything from paints to rags and bits of paper, write a story just for yourself (try writing out your dreams and turning them into short stories), make your own models without using a kit, cook without using recipes—the possibilities are endless. Just try turning on your imagination, and you'll find that you *are* creative.

Use your imagination in your schoolwork, too. On the next paper you're assigned, break the mold and deal with the topic in a whole new way. Think of as many questions as you can to ask about a day's worth of homework assignments, and see if that doesn't start a lot of interesting conversations. And when you're stuck for an idea about anything, from a homework problem to planning your future, don't hammer away at it. Instead, put it aside and do something else. The creativity in your unconscious will come up with a solution if you let it be for a while.

Let yourself daydream—it is when our minds are "wandering" that we are the most creative. Don't reject any of your "daydreaming" ideas—see about following up on some of them.

Remember that your mind tends to operate according to tried-and-true patterns: Whenever you break those patterns by doing anything in a way that is unusual for you, you are stretching your creativity. Remember, too, that in whatever you do well, you are already creative, so make the most of what you have by trying out even more new angles to your specialty.

SPEED
Speed is also an important aspect of brain power. To develop the quickness of your mind, take any of the exercises and suggestions above and gradually build up your speed in working through them. Just

as your strength builds gradually with physical exercise, your mental agility will increase when you keep practicing and working on quickness and accuracy.

"Make the most of what you have." That advice has been repeated, and it's important. One part of your brain can "teach" another how to do something, so take a look at the results of your self-tests in the last chapter and think of ways in which you can transfer knowledge and experience in one area to another one. Also, what you "have"—what you do well—should make you proud. Think in terms of what you do well, and you will find that you feel more confident in trying out the things you feel shakier about.

(8)

Making the Best of Your Brain

Making the most of what you have inside your head is important, especially because not everyone is good at everything. If your body is simply not suited for sports, for instance, you are not likely to become a star athlete. If you've developed a brain that is extra-sensitive in the right-sided, intuitive, and nonverbal areas, you may not be able to excel as a logical, rational thinker. But to make the most of yourself, you can adapt. (Remember that intelligence is goal-directed, adaptive behavior.)

Sally may really want to get involved in sports, but she doesn't have the skill. With her people-winning ways, though, she would make a terrific cheerleader. Someone else in the same situation might become a sports writer or be the team manager.

Jennifer may lack the skill to be an artist herself, but she can use her book smarts to read and learn as much about her favorite form of art as she can. Or if she can't make her hands do what she would like, she can express her creativity by writing.

Just because you're good at one thing doesn't mean you can't become involved in totally different forms of activities. We will all always be better in some areas than in others, because of the heredity that has physically shaped our bodies and brains, and because of the experiences that have guided our motivations, but we all have many directions in which we can choose to develop skill and from which we can find reward. Winston Churchill won fame as a world leader, but he also painted pictures. Paul Newman is known as an actor, but he drives racing cars as well.

Think about all the things you'd like to do and then brainstorm all the ways you could get involved in those activities. In doing so, you'll develop new centers of strength.

Take Care

Whatever you choose to do, you will be using your head and that miracle inside it—your brain. And however you use your brain, you will make the best of it by taking good care of it. A brain that is damaged cannot be repaired: We do not grow new brain cells after we are born. Brains can be damaged when they are not properly nourished, or when they are banged about or flooded by harmful chemicals. That means that to keep your brainpower buzzing, you need to eat well, you need to protect your head in any kind of sports or other potentially hazardous activities, and you need to stay away from alcohol or other drugs that achieve their effect by altering the brain.

Perhaps the *best* way to take care of your brain is to keep using it. Whatever brain cells you choose to exercise, it's important to keep exercising as many as you can. Recent research shows that the more people use their minds and brains, the longer they will be able to do so: Learning can continue throughout life, and intelligence can grow well into old age. All that learning requires is the linking up of neurons. Those linkages require only motivation and practice, so that —if you get into the habit now of using your head— you will find more ways, now and as you grow, of being smart.

In the beginning of this book, we asked some questions:

What *is* intelligence?

Is it the sum of an almost countless number of buzzing connections taking place within a small organ inside the skull?

Is it a mysterious quality like "mind" or "soul" that appears from an unknown source?

Is it a definite object, born into us and derived from our ancestors?

Does it grow with us, starting as nothing and developing within our environment as our bodies do?

Is it:

All of the above?
Some of the above?
None of the above?

Humans may well be the only creatures who try to understand themselves. Today, human research into the nature of intelligence and the workings of the human brain is proceeding at such a rapid pace that, between the time this book was written and the time it was printed, scientists came closer to detailed answers to those questions. Between the time the book was printed and the time it reached the shelf, too, they gained new knowledge—even, perhaps, between the time you began reading it and the time you finished.

The brain and the mind, though, are so complex that almost every new answer brings new questions —which bring new answers, and new questions, and . . . .

So far, the best answer to *our* question—What is intelligence?—is: "All of the above." But even more important than getting answers is asking questions, because that is what keeps our brains in gear. Each of us has different questions to ask, to answer, and to ask again: Each of us is intelligent in our own way, and we will stay smart if, in our own way, we keep using our heads.

(9)

Refresh Your Recollection

This list may help you to understand better the meaning of some of the more significant terms you've found in *Using Your Head*. Going through the list can also help you to review and remember some of the new facts and ideas you have picked up while reading through the book.

accommodation A style of learning and problem-solving that emphasizes intuition, active experimentation, and use of concrete experience.

aptitude A natural or inborn ability to learn or perform in a particular area, as an *aptitude* for art.

axon An extension of a nerve cell that transmits signals from the cell body to another cell. In the brain, axons are quite short, but in other areas of the nervous system, they may extend as much as a yard to reach the next nerve cell.

brain The organ contained within the skull, made up of nerve cells; the center of the nervous system. In humans, the brain weighs about three pounds and consists of about 100 billion specialized cells that control conscious and unconscious thought and the functions of all other bodily organs and systems.

brain stem The portion of the brain closest to the spinal column and serving as the main pathway for signals controlling conscious and unconscious physical activity. Part of the hindbrain, and sometimes used to mean the hindbrain.

cerebellum The "little brain," a large bulge on the back of the hindbrain. The cell systems in this, the second largest segment of the brain, are responsible for physical balance and coordination and perhaps for emotional development.

cerebrum The largest portion of the brain, divided into lobes and hemispheres containing nerve tissues that control such "higher" functions as sensations, conscious thought, and voluntary actions.

chromosome A portion of the nucleus of a cell that carries characteristics of that cell when it reproduces; essential in the transmittal of hereditary features from one generation to another.

cognition The overall process of knowing, thinking, or learning, including perception, memory, imaging, and judgment.

convergence A style of learning or problem solving that focuses on specialization and the narrow solutions to problems.

cortex The outer layer of the brain, especially the

cerebrum, where, it is thought, most of the higher mental activities, including thought, take place.

creativity The mental ability to produce new ideas or new solutions to old problems through the use of imagination or the combination of a variety of thought processes.

dendrites Hairlike fibers that cover the axons of nerve cells and that receive signals from neighboring cells.

divergence A style of learning or thinking with an emphasis on imagination and people skills.

electrochemistry The combination of electrical impulses with chemical changes that results in the transmission of energy, as from one part of the nervous system to another.

environment Surroundings. In relation to learning, intelligence, and development, the entirety of influences that operate outside an individual, as opposed to internal makeup or heredity.

forebrain The area of the brain including the cerebral hemispheres and the structures within them, such as the thalamus, hypothalamus, and optic nerves.

gene The carrier of a particular hereditary characteristic within the chromosomes of a cell.

hemisphere One "half" of the cerebrum. Not literally a half-globe, as the word itself means, but a major division of the cerebrum, united with the opposite hemisphere by connections deep within the cerebral core.

heredity The transmission of physical or mental characteristics from parents to child through the genes and chromosomes in the reproductive cells.

hindbrain The portion of the brain within the lower rear portion of the skull and including the top of the spinal column. In humans, it is the most basic and primitive part of the brain, controlling such essential processes as the transmission of sensory signals.

hormones Chemicals produced by glands within the brain and, under the control of the brain, elsewhere in the body. These chemicals regulate temperature, hunger, growth, and other conditions within the body, including functions of the brain itself.

hypothalamus A region of the midbrain whose functions include the regulation of temperature, appetite, and thirst.

instinct A natural, inherited impulse, in humans usually associated with our animal natures, as the *instinct* to flee from danger.

intellectual Having to do with the mind or reason rather than the emotions, instincts, or will.

intelligence The ability to learn, understand, and solve new problems. The use of the brain to achieve goal-directed, adaptive behavior.

intuition Judgments made or knowledge gained apparently without the use of conscious thought or reason.

IQ Abbreviation for "intelligence quotient," a ratio

of mental age, as measured by intelligence tests, to chronological age; sometimes used to rate intelligence. "IQ" also sometimes serves as shorthand for "intelligence."

learning The acquisition of knowledge or skill, usually through the general process of stimulus, response, and reward. The ease or success of learning depends upon the degree of motivation and amount of practice.

lobes In the cerebrum, rounded segments created as the developing brain doubles back on itself to fit the space within the skull. Each of the four major cerebral lobes contains cells specialized for different functions: Language seems to be concentrated in the frontal lobe, for instance, and important aspects of memory in parts of the parietal, temporal, and occipital lobes.

memory The storage of information in the brain. Though the exact locations and processes of memory are not known for certain, it appears that information is stored in three stages—immediate, short term, and long term—and is recalled through a complex series of trigger mechanisms.

midbrain The part of the brain connecting the central portions of the forebrain with the top of the brain stem, serving primarily as a relay station for signals sent among other brain segments.

mind A nonscientific word referring to mental activities in general, including conscious and unconscious thought, memory, reason, and opinion.

motivation The drive or impulse behind an action or behavior. In learning, a person may be *motivated* by the desire for a reward or the urge to avoid punishment.

neocortex The outermost layer of the cerebral cortex and the most recently developed part of the brain in terms of evolution. It is believed to be the site of some of the most sophisticated and abstract functions of the human brain. Sometimes used as a synonym for the cerebral cortex as a whole.

nervous system The entire network of the body's nerve cells, which send and receive electrochemical signals, via the spinal cord, between the control centers in the brain and every cell, tissue, organ, and system in the body.

neurons Nerve cells. Different from other cells in the body in the extensions (the axons) of the cell body which exchange electrochemical signals.

neuroscience The study of the body's nerves and nervous system with emphasis on the relationship of the nerves to intelligence, learning, and behavior.

organ A physical structure that performs a specific function within the body. Specialized cells make up tissues which combine to form organs. The brain is an organ, as are the stomach, heart, lungs, and other essential portions of the body's systems.

perception The receiving of information gathered by the senses and then interpreted in the brain, either automatically or by means of conscious or unconscious thought.

pineal A gland at the center of the midbrain whose actions control growth and development, among other functions.

problem solving A basic part of the thinking and learning processes, since both thinking and learning require the application of old and new information toward understanding and adapting to situations presented to the brain by the senses.

psychiatry The branch of medicine that studies and treats emotional, mental, and behavioral problems.

psychology Literally, the study of the mind ("psyche"), not neccessarily in a medical context; the study of behavior, mental processes, and emotional states of individuals or groups.

soul A nonscientific word referring either to all of the nonintellectual and nonphysical activities of a human being, such as emotions and "spirit," or to those aspects of humanity *plus* the workings of the conscious and unconscious mind—all of which are now thought to be centered somewhere in the brain.

synapse The connection point between two neurons: a tiny gap between the cells, filled with a chemical that transmits the electrical signals from one cell to the other.

thalamus A mass of cells in the midbrain whose primary function is to coordinate signals from the senses and to the muscles.

thinking A general term for the chain reactions of ideas that take place within the conscious and unconscious centers of the brain; separate from linkages of purely physical stimuli and reactions.

unconscious mind Those mental processes which occur without one's being aware of them.

(10)

Stretch Your Mind

Books

If you want to know more about your head, how it works, and how to use it, try some of the books listed here. Some are general; some are specific. Some are harder reading than others; some are easy. You should be able to find most of them in your library, and if you can't find what you're looking for, ask your librarian.

Aero, Rita, and Elliot Weiner, Ph.D. *The Mind Test.* New York: Morrow, 1981.
> A workbook of over three dozen self-scoring personality, aptitude, and psychological tests.

Albrecht, Karl. *Brain Power.* Englewood Cliffs, N.J.: Prentice-Hall, 1980.
> Information, guidance, and exercises designed to improve thinking skills. Aimed at adults, but useful and fun.

Bailey, Ronald H., et al. *The Role of the Brain.* New

York: Time-Life, 1975.

A clear presentation of the source of thoughts, feelings, and behavior.

Barth, George F. *Your Aptitudes: You Do Best What You Are Fitted to Do.* New York: Lothrop, Lee & Shepard, 1974.

A beginner's guide to exploring one's talents.

Bellezza, Francis S. *Improve Your Memory Skills.* Englewood Cliffs, N.J.: Prentice-Hall, 1982.

A psychologist explains memory and the various ways to develop it.

Berger, Melvin. *Exploring the Mind and Brain.* New York: Crowell, 1983.

Descriptions of recent discoveries in brain research.

Blakemore, Colin. *Mechanics of the Mind.* Cambridge University Press, 1977 (Reprint: 1983).

Explanation of how such functions as memory and language work.

Campbell, David P. *If You Don't Know Where You're Going, You'll Probably End Up Someplace Else.* Allen, TX: Argus Communications, 1974.

A good, short book to start you thinking on what you want out of life.

Cohen, Daniel. *Re-Thinking.* New York: Evans, 1982.

A guide to learning how to think, meant for adults, but of practical value for any age.

Diagram Group. *The Brain: A User's Manual.* New York: Coward, 1982.

A compact and thorough illustrated reference book on the anatomy and workings of the brain, its effects on the rest of the body, and influences on it.

Gallant, Roy A. *Memory: How It Works and How to Improve It.* New York: Four Winds Press, 1980.

A young person's guide to the workings of memory and ways to improve it.

Gilbert, Sara. *Ready, Set, Go: How to Find the Career That's Right for You.* New York: Four Winds Press, 1979.

The author's career-choosing guide includes several sections on exploring aptitudes and interests and describes many intelligence and personality tests.

Goldenson, Robert M. *All About the Human Mind.* New York: Random House, 1963.

An easy-to-read discussion by a psychologist.

Haines, Gail Kay. *Brain Power: Understanding Human Intelligence.* New York: Watts, 1979.

A basic book for young people.

Harth, Erich. *Windows on the Mind.* New York: Morrow, 1982.

A thick book, but one that clearly explains the relationships between brain, mind, and consciousness.

Raudsepp, Eugene. *More Creative Growth Games.* New York: Perigee, 1980.

Exercises for stretching your imagination.

Sagan, Carl. *The Dragons of Eden.* New York: Random House, 1977.

A fascinating exploration of human intelligence and its possible origins.

Taylor, David A. *Mind.* New York: Simon and Schuster, 1982.

A long book by an experimental psychologist that explores the mysteries of intelligence and includes puzzles and games to help explain some of the brain's processes.

This list will get you started. You might also want to browse through the shelves of your library or bookstore to find other titles, both informational and "how-to," that can help you expand your mind, explore your talents, and exercise your brain.

Other Resources

If you would like an in-depth look at *your* many ways of being smart, you might want to seek counseling or specialized testing, but it's important that you get it from reliable sources. Your school guidance counselor can advise you, and you can also get information from these organizations:

American School Guidance Association
American Personnel and Guidance Association
5203 Leesburg Pike

Falls Church, VA 22046

American Psychological Association
1200 17th Street, NW
Washington, DC 20036

National Education Association
1201 16th Street, NW
Washington, DC 20036

National Institute of Education
400 Maryland Avenue, SW
Washington, DC 20024

In the meantime, why not do some exploring on your own? If you have talents or skills for which you want to find outlets, or if you want to develop some new ones, join some new clubs at school or check out what's going on at your local "Y" or community center. You have many ways of being smart, and *lots* of places to use your talents and your head.

Index